bum into God

bumping into God

35 stories of finding Grace in unexpected places

Dominic Grassi

LOYOLAPRESS.

CHICAGO

LOYOLAPRESS.

3441 N. ASHLAND AVENUE
CHICAGO, ILLINOIS 60657

© 1999 Dominic Grassi
All rights reserved

All Scripture quotations are from the Jerusalem Bible © 1966
by Darton Longman & Todd, Ltd., and Doubleday, a division
of Bantam Doubleday Dell, Inc. Reprinted by permission.

Some of the stories in this book appeared in a different version
in *Markings* magazine.

Cover design by WATCH! Graphic Design
Cover art by Bruno Watel
Author photo by Barbara Zeman
Interior design by Lisa Buckley

Library of Congress Cataloging-in-Publication Data
Grassi, Dominic.
   Bumping into God : 35 stories of finding grace in unexpect-
ed places / Dominic Grassi.
        p.   cm.
   Originally published : Chicago : Loyola Press, 1999.
   ISBN 0-8294-1654-4 (pbk.)
   1. Christian life—Catholic authors. I. Title.
BX2350.3 .G73 2001
242—dc21
                                           00-048126
                                              CIP

Printed in the United States of America
00 01 02 03 04 / 10 9 8 7 6 5 4 3 2 1

contents

IF YOU HAVE HAD AN EXPERIENCE of bumping into God and would be willing to share it with Father Grassi for his next book, please send it to him c/o Trade Editorial Department, Loyola Press, 3441 N. Ashland Ave., Chicago, IL 60657.

introduction

I LIKE PEOPLE EVEN WHEN THEY BECOME AN overwhelming crowd. I'm attracted to art fairs, festivals, and wherever people gather and are unafraid of being themselves. People fascinate me. They surprise me. They lift me up and they bring me down. What I can expect is only the unexpected. They make me laugh when I should be crying. They leave me silent when I should be speaking. And they make me nod my head in the affirmative when I should be saying no.

Watching people helps me get in touch with myself, grounds me in what is truly real, and heightens my already tightly strung Italian feelings. You have to know that being Italian, I *feel* before any other response is possible. And being Italian, I naturally want to celebrate what I just felt.

That's the way it is, both a curse and a blessing. For many of us, the celebration usually involves food, a whole lot of food. Once I gave a daylong workshop to a parish that had been created by the merging of three smaller churches on how to be a welcoming community. An elderly woman who had been earnestly taking notes on everything I said came up to me during one of the breaks and exclaimed as I was biting into a bagel, "My goodness! You sure do a lot of eating at your parish." She was right. That's just a natural way for me to bring people together. I feel that what you are about to read will go well with a nice snack.

And so it is that my life is necessarily colored by strong feelings, formed by a celebration of the human spirit. These feelings are what ultimately drew me to the priesthood, and what I have, for over a quarter of a century, been privileged to share with so many people. And being Italian I also have a deep compulsion to share what I see with anyone who will stop and listen. You must remember that we Italians love to make what we experience bigger than life. Of this I unashamedly plead guilty, but I am unrepentant. For us, just about anything can become a Puccini opera.

So this, in an almond shell, is how this book came to be. If there is grace in any of it, it is caught up in the mystery of the wonderful people about whom I write. This is because they are God's loving presence connecting with me. For this reason, I want so much to share them with you. They are the grace that God has for whatever reason chosen to freely give to me and that I found myself compelled to share freely with you.

This is not a book of theology. But I hope it is a spiritual book. I hope it helps you celebrate God's love for you and all the people in your days and years. This is not a book about ideologies, but about people. I hope these people will bless you as they have me.

If you were standing right next to me, our shoulders touching, and you saw and heard everything and everyone along with me, you probably would not recognize your experience in my words when you read them. I don't set before you right or wrong words. I merely offer the glimpses God has offered me of grace, forgiveness, laughter, and all the rich blessings of life. They are glimpses gained during ordinary days, while in the midst of doing the mundane things I do.

Please feel free to use these reflections in any way you like for yourself or for others. Go ahead and retell these stories. Adopt them. Feel free to tear them to shreds. They are for you. But even better, why don't you start looking more closely at your own world. There are miracles and ordinary moments to celebrate, grace and joy to share, silly folk and saints to relish.

Your own stories, once they are set down in front of you, may astound you or at least humble you and make you pause and think and perhaps (surprise) say a little prayer. Who knows? Perhaps yours could be the second volume of a long series of stories about bumping into God. Or maybe they will become a treasure just for you, your pearl of great price.

Stories of God's Presence

People look for God's presence in many places. They gather in the basilicas of Rome or at the red rocks in Sedona. I find God's presence quite nearby—in the magnificent complexity of the human person. Are we not, after all, made in the image of our God? This God lovingly created us and walks with us still. Walks with the priest and the rabbi. Is present in the

Meanwhile the eleven disciples set out for Galilee, to the mountain where Jesus had arranged to meet them. When they saw him they fell down before him, though some hesitated. Jesus came up and spoke to them. He said, "All authority in heaven and on earth has been given to me. Go, therefore, make disciples of all the nations; baptize them in the name of the Father and of the Son and of the Holy Spirit, and teach them to observe all the commands I gave you. And know that I am with you always; yes, to the end of time."

~ **MATTHEW 28:16–20**

courage of two elderly sisters, the faith of a simple worker, or the innocence of a street person. We don't have to look very far to find God's presence brilliantly reflected.

two
priests

WHEN I WAS GROWING UP IN THE FIFTIES, Chicago was still divided into distinct neighborhoods. And quite often those neighborhoods were designated by parishes. So if someone asked where you were from, the easiest response would be "St. Bonnie's" or "Mary of the Lake" or "Tommy More." This immediately located you and in some instances communicated your ethnic background as well.

Our Lady of Mount Carmel was originally the Irish parish, the mother church of the neighborhood that was the suburb of Lakeview and is now a part of the trendy Near North Side. Big, beautiful homes with front yards and backyards and New York City–sized apartments have since given way to high-rises, four-plus-ones, and town homes. The area has become quite eclectic. But back then it was a classic neighborhood.

Our family was the only Italian one on our block. In school there were precious few others.

There were some Hispanics, including a number of Cuban refugees and other nationalities. But the Irish were still in the majority, including many of the priests in the rectory and most of the Sisters of Mercy who staffed the school.

The rich parishioners along Sheridan Road and Lake Shore Drive guaranteed good collections and a solvent operation even as the parish's western boundaries saw an increasing growth in less affluent minorities. Still, the parish would have been considered a plum assignment. The castlelike rectory always housed four or five priests, including a pastor, a senior associate, a newly ordained, and a resident or two whose main ministry was outside the parish.

When people ask me why I wanted to become a priest and when I first considered it, I immediately think of a particular priest. He was a resident who taught at the minor seminary downtown. His homilies made people laugh and reflect. He always seemed to be smiling. We kids would gather around him after Sunday Mass, and he made us laugh. He actually listened to us and was concerned about us. Fr. Gene Faucher was a good priest.

It was his example that convinced me to attend the seminary where he taught. It was he who was a support for all the teens in the parish. He was the one who stepped in when I got into some serious trouble with the disciplinarian at school. He also taught me a little Latin. But, most important, he taught me a lot about having integrity, and he inspired me to serve people by accepting them for who they are.

While this priest was at the parish, another priest arrived as a newly ordained associate. It was clear, at least in his own mind, that he was on a fast track, and having this parish as a first assignment was a sure sign of the greater heights for which he was poised.

He never liked my brothers or me, among others who were not Irish. He was in charge of the altar servers and made his displeasure known when each of us was elected Supreme Grand Knight of the Altar (how's that for a title!) by our peers over his candidates of choice.

My brothers and I didn't realize this until years later, when we compared notes after a few glasses of wine. This priest had taken me off the altar of the wedding of a young lay teacher who had asked me to be one of her servers. Then he suspended me for not handling the incense respectfully at a novena where none of the other three servers had shown up, and I was stuck trying to balance the thurible and boat (incense holder) by myself (I ended up spilling it on the Oriental rug after charring my fingers).

He left the priesthood a short time later.

The other priest went on to be a highly beloved pastor who, through his gentle care and concern, offered many years to the work of bringing people closer to God. He retired without much fanfare, and his ministry continued.

One day, I heard that the other man was re-applying for active ministry. This made a lot of his contemporaries happy. But I discovered how hard unconditional forgiveness really is. The Eucharist is a sign of unity. Could I ever bring myself to celebrate it with someone who had treated my family and me so poorly? I'll never know. He died of a heart attack before he was allowed to celebrate Mass once again.

Recently, now-retired Gene Faucher and I were invited to the dinner of mutual friends. I was so grateful for the opportunity—in the midst of our shared stories and reminiscences—to thank him for the tremendous impact he had on my life. He seemed genuinely surprised at what I said. We don't thank others nearly enough for all that they have done for us.

That experience also helped me let go of the hurts from the other priest that, even after his death, were still weighing me down. After all, I learned from both of them, in profoundly different ways, what it means to be a good priest. And, inspired by both their examples, I now try hard to be the best priest I can be. Perhaps a young man or woman with whom I have worked will one day decide to serve God as a priest. That person, too, will owe something to both the priests who influenced me so profoundly.

God's presence comes to us in many ways. Sometimes the most difficult of situations can become sacramental moments whereby God touches our lives in a way that guarantees we will never be the same again. We cannot expect to find God only in the beautiful. Sometimes we find God in the most unlikely people or places. Our task is to look—and look again. What a lost opportunity if we fail to see the God who is so near to us.

the
quiet teacher

OUR NEIGHBORHOOD WAS LOUD. THE BACKYARDS
and porches and alleys seemed to make shouting
back and forth a natural thing. The ragman came
around on Mondays yelling, "Old clothes for sale!"
which always confused me because he wanted to buy
clothes, not sell them. The big, red vegetable truck
stopped by later in the week, and from the back of it
the driver sang a medley of what he had that day:
"We got peppers and bananas and melons of all
kind." The knife sharpener was the most pragmatic,
cutting through the confusion with his "Time to
sharpen your knives."

Combine all that with the bells from the
ice-cream carts, dads sitting in their Chryslers or
Oldsmobiles listening to the radios until they fell
asleep, mothers calling out back doors or windows for
their children, who were themselves screaming, "Alle,
alle, oxen free" at the top of their lungs to signal the

end of a game of sardines. If you wanted to be heard, you yelled. I figured that we noisy Italians had a distinct advantage in this area!

Across the alley lived a Jewish family. The father was a rabbi at the large synagogue on Sheridan Road. Unlike the rest of us, he never raised his voice. In fact, when he spoke to us kids it was barely above a whisper, even when one of our foul balls crashed its way into his bedroom through the closed window. His patience with us, his calmness—but most of all his being so quiet—made me really nervous. I felt as though he could read my thoughts.

One of his two children was a son whose name was Hillel. We spent a lot of time playing together. On Friday evenings this could be inconvenient, especially in the winter when darkness came early, because Hillel had to be home before sundown on Fridays. One time his mother, looking distressed, asked if I could do her a favor. It was Friday and already dark outside. The Sabbath had begun, and she had left the burners of her gas stove on. Could I please turn them off for her? Even as a youngster I was impressed by how serious they were about their religion. She gave me some cookies to take home and share with my brothers. They were salty and sweet at the same time. My brothers would have liked them, if the cookies had made it that far.

Depending on what game we kids in the neighborhood were playing, sometimes we gathered in the sandy lot next to our house, sometimes on Pine Grove Avenue, occasionally in our big backyard, but never in Hillel's yard. The owners of their building had paved it and turned it into a parking area for three cars, one for each of the three apartments.

Once a year in the autumn, the rabbi would move his car and carefully construct a beautiful tent (we called it a fort) out of pipes and the heaviest plastic he could find. Its roof was made of plastic-lined bamboo poles. It never leaked, and it had kind of an exotic look about it. From the ceiling he hung apples and pomegranates and grapes. His family would gather there and celebrate the holy days, eating their meals and praying. From our house we could see the glow of the candles through the frosted plastic.

This tent would have been the perfect target for vandalism. At the very least we could have sneaked in and stolen the fruit. But every year the rabbi called us over just when he finished constructing the tent. Standing there in his sweaty T-shirt, he would invite us, as Hillel's friends, to have some cookies and juice. He quietly explained to us how important the holy days were to him and his family. We ate and listened politely even if we didn't fully understand him.

He explained that he needed our help. Would we watch over the tent when they were not around so that nobody could damage it? He always made it sound as if our messing it up was the furthest possibility from his mind. In return he promised to keep the tent up for a full month after the holy days ended so that we could use it as a fort. He didn't have to remind us that there would also be a party for us the day before he took it down.

We guarded that tent with our lives. Nobody but nobody could set foot inside it without the rabbi's permission until the holy days were over. Once, when we woke up and found a piece of the plastic flapping in the breeze as if it had been purposely cut, we tried desperately to tape it back together. When the rabbi saw us, he chuckled—even his laughter was soft—and told us not to worry, that the wind had ripped that piece and he was going to replace it.

So each year for a month we had a grand time playing cops and robbers, Indians and cowboys, Flash Gordon versus Ming the Merciless, or whatever other games we could create. We also learned a little about the fine art of compromise and how good win-win situations could be.

In his quiet way, the rabbi taught us the more important lesson of tolerance, how to treat one another with the respect we wanted shown to us and how it was possible to bring out the best in each other. His was the wisdom of the Old Testament patriarchs, the strength of the prophets, and the cunning of the judges. It is not surprising that *rabbi* means teacher.

We learned that there can be a sacred space where God's presence is felt in a special way. We learned that what made the space sacred was our willingness to want God to be present and to respect that presence. In the most subtle of ways, we learned that God's presence can most often be found inside our very selves when we rise to the occasion and are the best that we can be.

a bookstore
one flight
down

A SHORT WHILE BACK, I ATTENDED AN
overnight workshop at the seminary where I had
received my training. I found myself with a free
evening and set out for the local shopping mall. It
had been a chicken farm back when I was a seminarian. Time really does change things. After some
aimless wandering through stores filled with items
of no importance to me, I ended up in a bookstore.
It was a typical store, but for me it conjured up a
long-buried image from my youth.

I remembered a cozy, crowded basement shop,
one flight underground. It was run by two elderly sisters who I am convinced had personally selected
each title that was on their overflowing shelves.

What I walked into this evening was a two-story
(complete with twin escalators) megastore containing
tens of thousands of books, tapes, cards, magazines,
and gifts neatly placed on dust-free shelves. Lush chairs

had been strategically placed throughout the store to accommodate people weary from looking at so many books in a single place on a single evening. People lounged in those chairs and read as though they were in a library, not a store, oblivious to everyone and everything around them. There was even a built-in coffee shop in the center of the store. I purchased five books, two cookies, and a carton of 2 percent milk.

As I sat there looking around and enjoying my snack, I thought of the little basement bookstore of my childhood. Now, we kids in the neighborhood didn't actually go in this store to buy books. There was no children's or juvenile section. We all had library cards anyway. We went to the bookstore to buy a single playing card with the painting of a beautiful horse or the picture of an antique car or railroad engine on the back. Depending on our selection, we paid two cents to a staggering one dollar each. We bought our cards and then traded them among ourselves. The owners of the bookstore did have their rules. We were never allowed to open a new deck of cards. But we were free to browse through the partial decks from which cards had already been sold. I remember most vividly the smell, look, and feel of that little shop. Today the only words I can use to describe it are *clean* and *safe*.

One day when I was about ten years old, I was in the shop trying to make the very difficult decision of whether to purchase two matching cards at fifty cents each—one the picture of a white stallion entitled "Daybreak" and the other a picture of a striking black mare called "Midnight"—or to go up to the gyp joint and buy a bunch of baseball cards. Before I could make up my mind, I overheard a customer talking to the two elderly sisters. I saw him holding a book up over his head. It looked like a calculating, menacing pose. I don't remember the exact name of the book, but I do recall that it was a Jewish cookbook because I had whispered to Merle, my first-ever girlfriend who was with me and who was Jewish, that if he didn't buy the book she should get her mom to buy it.

But as the man's voice grew louder and more enraged, I realized that he was threatening to burn down the bookstore if the owners insisted on selling books about Jews (except he used all sorts of words I had never heard before but could sense were not nice names for Jewish people). By some instinct I tried to shield Merle from this man. But at that point he threw the book onto the floor and stormed up the stairs and out of the little shop, trailing threats behind him. After a few moments of all of us just standing there quietly, the shop began to feel clean and safe again.

I wondered what the two elderly ladies would do. They had not said a word during the man's tirade. With a single and almost imperceptible nod to the other, one of them picked up the book, gently straightened out its jacket, and placed it back on the shelf where anyone could see it. Neither of them spoke a word, but it was clear they were not about to be intimidated.

Merle and I left the shop, ran back to her home, and breathlessly told her mother what had happened. She listened with a sad expression that slowly hardened into defiance. She took off her apron, grabbed her purse, and walked over to the little bookstore with the two of us tagging along behind her. This was an adventure! She greeted the ladies with a smile and asked if they happened to have a Jewish cookbook. She bought that book then and there, along with two or three other volumes that she picked up after barely looking at their titles. As we were leaving the store the owners called Merle and me over to them and let each of us pick out any two cards we wanted.

That incident came back to me clearly as I sat there eating a better-than-average oatmeal raisin cookie. I am sure that these days there are corporate policies that determine which books are selected for such large stores—policies based on demographics or sales projections or profit margins and the like. And I am sure that when complaints come in about a particular title, someone from the home office sends a form letter covering all the legal and diplomatic bases.

I am equally certain that little bookstores down one flight of stairs are becoming extinct. And gone with them are the genuine heroes and heroines who loved the printed word so much, who rejected bigotry and hatred so that every book on their cramped shelves was a true symbol of freedom and openness. For them the bottom line was the enjoyment, excitement, challenge, humor, pathos—in short, the truth of the message. That is why their little shops were such special, sacred places.

Before I left the big store and the mall with my discounted books in a plastic bag, I picked out a nice Jewish cookbook and bought it in honor of the two elderly sisters and their very important little bookstore one flight down.

We often try to force God's presence into the large, dramatic cathedrals of the world. But, as you walk down the street in your neighborhood, listen closely for evidence of God's goodness, love, justice, safety, and peace. Be open to the courageous messages spoken—with or without words—among the people in your environment. God is surely right here, where you and your neighbors live. And his Word is surely present. It is inclusive and full of peace. It helps people keep up their journeys throughout the week—throughout their lives.

wisdom teeth and window washers

RECENTLY I HAD AN OPPORTUNITY (BUT ONE I would most certainly not wish to repeat) to reflect on God's presence in my life and how God can find simple ways to assure us that we are not alone.

There I was, sitting uncomfortably in a dentist's chair in an oral surgeon's office for over forty-five minutes before anyone came in to see me. Knowing that before the extraction of my four wisdom teeth I would have to have my blood pressure taken, I tried my best to remain calm. But as I listened to the strange and medieval sounds coming from another room, even prayer was failing me. When a nurse finally came in and took my blood pressure, I knew the doctor would not be pleased. And when I found out how high my blood pressure was, it only served to make me more tense. A vicious cycle was beginning, and I couldn't help it.

Then I looked out the windows at the high-rise across the street and noticed that two window washers, supported by nothing more than ordinary-looking ropes and harnesses, were quickly and expertly working their way down the fifty-story tower. I sensed God showing me that indeed there was some other place I would rather not be than in this dentist's chair. And I realized that there is always something more frightening and dangerous than the situation you may find yourself in at the moment.

I stopped worrying. I sensed that God was with me. And so I relaxed.

After a fifteen-minute wait, the doctor finally walked in. He saw the blood-pressure reading on my chart and was not pleased. But with confidence I invited him to take it again; I said that it would be better. He did, and it was.

Two and one-half painful hours later all four teeth had been extracted. As I looked across the street I saw that the window washers were finally on ground level. I had been following their progress to keep my mind from what was happening in my mouth. I had the distinct feeling that they were in better shape than I was.

In no condition to drive home, I waited in front of the dentist's office for my ride to pick me up. One of the washers came across the street to put his equipment into a truck parked nearby. I walked over to him with my mouth still frozen with Novocain and packed with gauze. I must have looked and sounded strange. He didn't understand me at first when I asked him how he came to be employed as a high-rise window washer. So I tried to speak more clearly. When he finally realized what I was asking, he told me how good God had been to him.

Before this job, he had been mostly unemployed or earning minimum wage. Now he was making enough money to support his family. I asked him if the height and the danger frightened him. He said that he felt God would protect him and that he had nothing to worry about. Looking at my face, he asked what my problem was. I told him that I just had four teeth pulled. He literally ran off with his hand protectively covering his mouth, exclaiming that no one would ever do that to him.

I rode home in the car quietly. It is not often that I have nothing to say. But the Novocain was beginning to wear off, and I was realizing that it was going to be a long night, even with painkillers. I would have lots of time to think about God's being there with me for something—let's face it—as inconsequential as the pulling of a few teeth. And at the same time he had been there for the window washer, protecting someone who was only trying to make an honest living.

How many countless others was God with at exactly the same time? Certainly there are innumerable people with problems and concerns far, far greater than mine and in far more dangerous situations than even the window washer's.

I am not sure how this assurance of God's personal care is accounted for by all the theology I have studied. But I am certainly relieved to have that kind of caring and present God to count on when I need help. And I hope that I will have the same faith at far more essential and important times in my life.

god has a name

IT'S HAPPENED TO ME BEFORE, BUT NEVER
twice in the same week. Sometimes I must be a little
dense, and God, who loves us with a great sense of
humor, must realize the only way to be present to
me is by figuratively hitting me over the head. This
time I was slugged and almost didn't know it.

Neither story made the headlines. In fact,
neither was mentioned in the papers at all. In the
constant ebb and flow of our busy neighborhood,
it all went completely unnoticed. Even our church,
busy with all its outreach and programs, failed to
take notice.

One of our street people was found dead in a
nearby alley one morning a short while back. I doubt
that anyone wept for him, and I wonder if anyone
will miss him. It's certainly easy to pass judgment on
him, talking of a wasted life or using the term *bum*

with indifference. But none of us ever got to know his story. And now we never will. Don't you think that when his mother held him as a baby in her arms, she had great hopes for him? Or did she resent his coming into the world? In either case, he was made in God's image.

Perhaps when he was a boy looking up at the clouds, he dreamed about his future, about all the good things that would come his way. Who knows? He might have left a wife and family, who do not even know his fate. Or maybe he died with an emptiness of heart that was never filled by another's love.

Had he ever been happy? Did he ever know contentment? Did he die angry at the hand life dealt him? Did he ever sense God's loving presence? We will never know. And that leaves me frustrated and more than a little sad. When the police came and took his body away, that was the end of it.

Kindhearted fellow that I am, I decided we should pray for this nameless person at Mass. So we added an intention to the prayers of the faithful. It was the topic of my pastor's column. And I preached my Sunday homily on the death of this stranger in our midst and its implications for all of us.

Most people would have ignored the whole situation. Very few would have found the gospel evident in it. In short, the nameless tragedy of that poor soul turned into a bonanza of triumphant proportions for me. Opportunity knocked and I took advantage of it.

It is amazing how blind and empty I really was. So caught up in my own success, so blinded by my own preaching pyrotechnics, I didn't even realize that I had no feelings for the dead man. He had just become a useful tool for me to display my talent as a preacher and a writer. At first, my intentions were fine. But using him as an object kept him the nameless street person in death that he had been in life. And keeping him nameless kept me from seeing God's presence in him. That was perhaps the greatest injustice. God, ever patient, would have to knock some sense into me. And so God did, without much delay.

Less than a week later, another of our street people came by the rectory looking for a handout and promptly fell asleep on the ledge outside the rectory door. With too much Wild Irish Rose in him, he spilled the soup I had given him. Nobody was around when he fell from the ledge about ten feet down to the concrete walkway below. I have to confess that when I initially saw what happened, I was angry about the noodles and carrots all over the rectory steps. But one look told me I had better call an ambulance. He had landed on his head and was too drunk to understand what had happened. The paramedics came quickly. They examined him. It was hard to tell the extent of his injuries. Even before he fell he was in no shape to communicate. They put a neck brace on him, strapped him to a stretcher, and drove him to the hospital.

After they left, I realized that I had talked with this person many times, given him pop or soup, even called the police on him once when he was so drunk I thought he would hurt himself. But I had never bothered to learn his name. I never saw God as God was being revealed to me in this man. I gave him a blessing and said a small prayer for him as they wheeled him away. I looked at the bit of blood staining the sidewalk and promised that if I ever saw him again, I'd find out his name.

About two months later he reappeared. I asked him his name. He would only volunteer "Bob." He was suspicious as to why I wanted to know it. When I asked Bob if he remembered what happened the day he got hurt, he assured me he did. He told me he had been attacked by four Italians with golf clubs. He wouldn't believe me when I told him he had fallen off the ledge. He made me laugh that day—as well as any time after that when I'd see him. After a few months, though, Bob disappeared. I don't know where he is or what has happened to him. But since he left I feel that God is a little less present to me.

I'll have to make sure that I'm looking closely for where God will reappear in my life. This is one of the important tasks given to us Christians.

Stories of God's Will

Just what does God want from us? And where do we find God's will for us? Sometimes it's as clear as a winter morning on a lake. Other times it is shrouded in the fog of our own unbelief. Often the search for God's will is more challenging than the action we must take once we've found it. It may appear in a

Jesus said: "I am the Way, the Truth and the Life. No one can come to the Father except through me. If you know me, you know my Father too. From this moment you know him and have seen him."

~ JOHN 14:6–7

child's game or in an old person's wisdom. The words of a strong Chicago cop or the laughter of a young granddaughter, even the sound of a whole different culture, may echo back to us what God wants us to do—as well as how we might do it.

goal
sticker

OUR BACKYARD FACED A HONEYCOMBED MAZE OF
streets and alleys connected by unlit gangways and
narrow passageways. It was all that an urban neighborhood should be. Some homes had porches, and,
depending on a porch's characteristics, it might have
a name, such as "the fort" or "the cheese hole."

Even now when I think of the old "cheese
hole" on Pine Grove Avenue I find myself shudder-
ing. The porch had been so named by a generation
of kids before us because the slabs of concrete making up its four walls were peppered with large holes.
It looked, to our imaginative young minds, like a
giant hollowed-out piece of Swiss cheese. The under-
side of that porch was like a cave—dark, with perpet-
ually moist and damp-smelling sand covering the
ground. That was because the cheese hole was where
kids went to the bathroom if, in the middle of playing, they didn't have time to go all the way home.

Not too long ago my older brothers finally confessed to me that when I was in my pre-memory stroller years, our mother would insist that they take me out to play with them. I am quite certain that I, as the youngest (and a spoiled) child, would not stop howling until they took me with them. After some spirited but futile protesting, my brothers would give in and wheel me out with them. Our mother, waving us on our way with a tomato-sauce-stained wooden spoon, would beam with pride at how her four boys got along so well together.

It was my oldest brother Joe's devious idea to wheel me, strapped tightly into my stroller, under the cheese hole and then leave me there where my cries could not be heard. Our mother, checking on us from the backyard, couldn't see my abandonment. After a couple of hours, my brothers would finally come for me and bring me home, but not before telling me to keep my mouth shut if I didn't want to be tied to my stroller and abandoned under the cheese hole for all eternity. I certainly was no dummy; I stayed quiet about it. It must have been a great day when I was finally allowed to play with the big kids on my own two feet and the old stroller was picked up by Goodwill. To this day, if I smell urine mixed with sand I break into a cold sweat. Thank God for odorless kitty litter, or I couldn't be a cat owner.

One of our alley games was the venerable, low-tech kick-the-can. I wonder if anyone plays that game nowadays. Back then, there was no greater sound than the clatter of the can being kicked, freeing us from standing around "in jail," unable to do anything but watch. We'd run off with a scream to hide again, this time certain that we'd never get caught.

Of course every kid wanted to be "it," to be the one who got to catch everyone in their hiding places and put them in jail. But this had to be done without anyone sneaking up to kick the can, sending the whole captured bunch off and running in glee. To be fair, we would "one potato, two potato" to select who got to be "it." It didn't matter much who that was—unless it was my best friend, Murray. Nobody ever wanted Murray to be "it" because he was always so afraid that someone would kick the can that he seldom moved more than a few feet away from it. This strategy worked; no one could ever beat him to the can. But then again, no one would get caught by him either because he refused to go far enough away from the can to find us. Inevitably the game would slow to a virtual standstill.

Frustrated, we would peek out from our hiding places and taunt him by chanting in singsong voices, "Goal sticker, goal sticker, Murray is a goal sticker!" Now that would get him plenty mad, and finally he'd come after us, loosening up the game and getting unnerved big time because someone would always run up and kick the can, freeing anyone he might have captured. This would cause him to sit on the can again and not move. We'd grow so tired of his behavior that it wasn't fun anymore. So we'd give up, leave our hiding places, and walk up to Berger's Drugstore for a chocolate phosphate.

No matter what we're doing, it's necessary to take some risks, at least occasionally. It's how we make discoveries and perfect inventions. It's how relationships deepen. It is definitely how kick-the-can should be played.

Who are the risk takers? Some of them are young people who on the first day of driver education want to be on the expressway. Workers on the low rungs of the corporate ladder take risks; it's the only way they can get noticed and climb higher. But it seems that, for too many people, the more steps they take, the fewer risks they take.

The disenfranchised have no choice but to take risks. After all, it's not CEOs or middle managers who go out on strike or lead a boycott or a march. Quite often the elderly are forced to take risks when they realize they have nothing—or everything—to lose. Elderly pope John XXIII was supposed to be an interim, caretaker pope. He sure fooled a lot of younger cardinals. Oscar Romero was named bishop precisely because the powers that be saw him as cautious and not a risk taker. He surprised everyone, even himself.

But there are just too many goal stickers around these days, people who won't stray from the can of their self-interest. I suggest that we all start shouting, "Goal sticker!" at politicians, business leaders, clergy, and anyone else—including ourselves—who won't risk doing the right thing.

Let's make a pact to take more risks. Let's take a chance and stray a little from certainty. Let's try doing things in a new way. We'll make some mistakes. The can will get kicked over, and we'll need to start again. But if we make a new discovery, if people become happier and more whole, if they come closer to God, then we've won the game. Winning when we could possibly lose—now that's exciting. But playing it safe will ultimately end the game.

God's will is expressed not through bolts of lightning but through our own actions—the risks we take and the ways in which we move away from what feels safe. For this, faith is necessary. But the return, given God's will, can be spectacular.

a new year's resolution kept

THERE'S A GENERATION OF PEOPLE OUT THERE,
sometimes patronizingly called "old-timers," who
have a genuine appreciation for how God's will
works in their lives. Jack is one of those people.

He first appeared almost magically at the steps
of the church a few years ago, waiting patiently for
me to unlock its thick wooden doors so that he could
come in a few moments before Mass to pray. He used
a tattered-beyond-recognition prayer book that he
took reverently from an old schoolbag-type satchel.
He carried the satchel in one hand, balanced by a
cane in the other. He told me he had just recently
moved into the subsidized senior housing building a
few blocks away. He was delighted that he could now
walk to church on his own.

Jack always tips his hat to me in a bygone,
courtly fashion. I must confess that it took me more

than a few weeks to understand much of his English, hidden as it was under a thick Irish brogue. And to this day there is always a warm greeting, some talk about the beautiful morning, and then a benediction ending with a warning to take care of myself.

Occasionally, Jack calls me over to him and furtively passes me a five-dollar bill hidden in a thick handshake. He always does this with the same apology, saying that he wishes it could be more. And then he suggests that I use the money to buy myself a good pair of socks. I wonder how Jack knows that I (like most priests I know) am always in need of good socks.

Last New Year's Day, I found myself preaching, without much enthusiasm, about making New Year's resolutions to become peacemakers, to help make God present in our world as Mary had done. After Mass, Jack stayed around to tell me his resolution. He was proud of it, and he wanted me to know what it was. Quite simply, he resolved to be alive next New Year's Day. With a wink and a proud smile, he said that he had been able to keep this resolution without fail for the last eighty-four years. I wished him luck and assured him that I'd be seeing him next year at this time.

Jack indeed made it to another New Year's Day. But the past year had been tough on him. During the spring, after missing Jack's early Sunday greeting for a couple of weeks, I grew worried about him. I found out that he had been hospitalized for bypass surgery. He was recovering at his son's home. I was pretty certain I would not see him again.

So I was more than a little surprised when Jack reappeared a month later at the steps of the church. He was thinner and a little less certain on his feet, but the same old Jack. When I asked how he was feeling, he simply thanked God "for being alive" and then admonished me to take care of myself.

Jack has become a very important part of my Sunday mornings. He is a grace and a blessing to me at the start of a usually hectic day. So it saddened me deeply when I heard that he is more ill than he knows. His family has decided, for whatever reason, not to reveal to Jack the seriousness of his situation. It is their choice, and it isn't my place to interfere.

I believe they are not being fair to Jack. I have a feeling that he would want to know the truth. But I have an even deeper feeling that he probably already does know and is merely playing along, kind and gentle man that he is. He would not want to hurt his family, but he is comfortable with his fate because he knows it is God's will.

Jack could teach his family a thing or two about God's will. We can't run from it or hide from it. And, most important, we shouldn't be afraid of it.

Ignoring it won't change it or make it go away. Like Jack, we should embrace each day as God gives it to us. We should set our goals, make our resolutions, and then let God do with us as God wills.

celebrating growth

THERE IS A PART OF ME THAT WILL ALWAYS BE a teacher. One of the joys I still experience at the start of a new school year is seeing all the growth in the children. There is the five-year-old who walks into the school confidently, with her backpack weighing almost as much as she does. She doesn't hesitate for a moment and wouldn't consider looking back over her shoulder at her mother. Last year she wouldn't leave her mother's side, clinging to her and crying. Now she is all grown up and ready to play with her friends. And look at that fourth grader. What was he fed over the summer? Is the human body really capable of growing six inches over two and a half months? And the eighth grader walks by, no longer a child but entering that awkward and embarrassing time called adolescence.

I'm sure that God wants us to keep growing long after our bodies reach a genetically predetermined point. It is God's will that we grow both as humans and as Christians through all the days allotted us. Too often growth goes unnoticed and uncelebrated. Right now I'd like to celebrate the growth of a particular person I know. He didn't grow in the way I wanted him to grow, but clearly God's direction and will are being accomplished in his life. The growth is real and filled with hope.

Recently he and I went to an authentic city deli that serves big, sloppy sandwiches because, in my mind, a cop always likes big, sloppy sandwiches. In any case, I like them. We only get together once or twice a year because of our busy schedules. I can't believe that he is now over thirty and married to the female police officer he dated for a few years. Looking at him left me wondering where all the time had gone.

I taught Pat in the high school seminary on the South Side of Chicago. He and his large family lived almost directly on the runway of Midway Airport. They had moved further west in the city because of racial changes in their former neighborhood. Like some other Southwest Siders, they carried their prejudices and anger with them when they moved. Pat was careful not to express those feelings around me. But when he was with people of like mind and opinion, his prejudices weren't far from the surface. I could see that there was a struggle going on inside of him.

Pat did not continue his studies for the priesthood after high school, as I had hoped he would. In fact, he didn't even go on to college. After a few meaningless jobs, he was accepted into the Chicago Police Department. From his first day on the force, he has loved being a Chicago cop. While I was disappointed at his not pursuing the priesthood, I hoped that he would become a good police officer: honest and fair, not puffed up with his own power and authority, and not too quick to use violence to solve conflicts.

We talked for a long time over the sloppy deli sandwiches. After a few years on the beat, Pat had been promoted to a position as a plainclothes officer in one of the toughest and most diverse districts in the city. It wasn't easy work, but he found it exciting. No one so young should have to face on a daily basis so much of what is truly sick and evil. But that's part of Pat's job. And, to my amazement, that is what has caused him to grow. As we visited I noticed that he no longer spoke with the mindless prejudices with which he grew up. He wasn't generalizing about people or putting them into categories. He seemed secure enough to realize that it was no longer necessary to lift himself up by putting others down.

This tough job has caused Pat to develop the valuable skill of distinguishing between the act and the person committing it. (Not too many of us are good at that.) All that he sees and experiences on a regular basis has forced him to become more reflective, because he knows that his only other option is to become callous and cynical. He is indeed savvy and street-smart. He knows how to protect himself and do his job well. But the fire of his daily experiences has burnt away all the prejudice that was such a part of who he used to be.

I continue to pray that God will shield my friend from harm in his dangerous work. And I pray that when he is old and gray he will tell his grandchildren how happy he was following God's call in his life. Yes, it *was* God's call and will—and not what I wanted Pat to do—that has made him grow into, and even beyond, his potential. God's will is the best thing we can do with our lives. Pat has helped me learn this lesson.

go fly
a kite

TRUSTING GOD IS ONE WAY WE GET THROUGH
the myriad of choices and opportunities that constantly face us. But trust is a virtue not much in style
these days. If someone says to you, "My, what a trusting person you are!" it can be taken in many different
ways. When we try to ascertain God's will, we don't
find a lot of support from our culture. If we trust anyone beyond ourselves, we must usually do it alone.

At this point in my life, it is very hard for me
to believe that I have an older brother who, as of this
writing, is already a grandfather three times over.
Seeing someone close to me reach such a milestone
reminds me of the doors that my choice to enter the
priesthood has closed finally and forever behind me.

How clearly I remember holding my brother's
oldest daughter in my arms, marveling at her three,
yes three, sets of dimples. There was one set on her
elbows. The other two were on areas we call cheeks.

She was the first of my nieces whose wedding I was privileged to celebrate. All too quickly she has grown up to be a wonderful young mother, married to a very nice young man. Their two children, my brother's first two grandchildren, quickly became very special to him. This was easy to see. I always knew when his grandchildren were coming for a visit, because those were the only times in the winter when his house was warm enough for me to feel the tip of my nose. (And with a nose like mine, that is always an important consideration.) All the hard work that my brother, consciously or not, had put into becoming the family curmudgeon absolutely melted in the presence of his two grandchildren. He would hold them and play with them and quite often was more animated around them than around any of the rest of us. It was an interesting transformation to watch.

But it all came screeching to a temporary halt when he learned that his daughter and his son-in-law and, most important, his two beloved grandchildren would be moving to Poland for two full years. It was a job opportunity they couldn't afford to pass up.

Again, given the limitations of my own experiences, I knew I couldn't appreciate the depth of his impending loss. I understood better when, a week before their departure, he looked at me and said, "Damn, I am going to miss my grandchildren so much. Why does this have to happen?" Then I observed him sitting back, almost trancelike, watching the children's every move, trying to soak it all in and capture their presence before they had to leave.

That was a lot for my brother to share with me, and I knew that I needed to respond. So I went to my car and took out a neon-colored kite I kept in the trunk for just such emergencies. When I brought it in I told my brother to get out his camera and his video recorder and meet his grandchildren and me in the park behind his house.

Fortunately, the wind cooperated. My brother took great pictures and videos of his two grandchildren happily flying a kite for the first time in their young lives. I watched him lighten up considerably as we continued to create sustaining images and memories. It became a fun afternoon, but it was something more as well. I felt good, knowing that I had given my brother something special even if I would never be in a position to appreciate fully what he has or to be blessed with grandchildren. I appreciated that in some small way I was able to share those feelings with him that afternoon.

I was left with the image of two little children excitedly holding on to a kite string, with no concern at all about their future. Their laughter still echoed inside me on the drive home as I reflected on just how much God's will is like flying a kite. Seemingly invisible forces determine whether or not a kite will become airborne. Those winds can grab hold of the kite so powerfully that they carry it to heights that are limited only by the length of the string. But just as quickly, those same forces can drop the kite into an irreversible tailspin. All of this is done in what appears to be an arbitrary, senseless pattern. But if we knew the laws of physics and the science of meteorology, there would be little, if any, mystery to what was happening. It also wouldn't be as fun.

No amount of scientific knowledge will help us know what God's will is for us. So we shouldn't always be asking about it and questioning it. Sometimes it is better just to go for the ride and trust those invisible winds. Sometimes we'll experience a sudden dip and end up in a tangle. Other times we will soar, worry-free, into the heavens. But even caught up in a tree, we are still as free as when we are flying into the clouds. Whatever the outcome, we shall soar again. We can trust God in this.

road maps and hardheads

THE REGION OF SOUTH CENTRAL ITALY FROM
which my family originated is called Bari. Its capital
city is also called Bari. (Before we chuckle, I suggest
that we all remember New York, New York.) The city
boasts a magnificent cathedral. In that cathedral lies
the body of none other than Saint Nicholas. There
are many legends and stories about how the remains
of a saint from Asia Minor were somehow trans-
ported to an Italian city across the Adriatic Sea. For
sure, tourism is never given as a reason. But a saint's
feast day leads to festivals, which lead to pilgrimages,
which lead to a booming economy. For me, it is just
plain fun thinking that the bones of Santa Claus are
there in the cathedral for all to come and venerate.

The people from this region are also known
throughout Italy for their incredible stubbornness.
When one admits to being from Bari, people may

well mutter, "Testa dura" (which means "hard head") and, with all four fingers touching the thumb, emphatically tap his forehead as a sign of obstinacy. I cannot claim the certainty of Santa Claus's tibia in the cathedral, but I will attest to what a stubborn people we are.

For centuries this stubbornness probably had little impact on the rest of the world. It no doubt led to some amazing domestic altercations. I am sure there were blood feuds that spanned generations, the cause of original conflict lost with the passing of time. Colorful colloquial phrases and gestures hint at just how stubborn these people can be. One of my favorites is used around chronic complainers. Loosely translated, it is: "I'm the one laying the egg, and you are the one saying you have the sore backside."

But the advent of the automobile has brought a new and terrifying dimension to life in Bari. I have spent most of my adult life driving in Chicago. I have driven throughout the U.S. as well, including the "Big Three" cities noted for their traffic: New York City, Washington, D.C., and Boston. I have driven in major metropolitan centers in Canada and Europe. But I must admit that never, ever have I experienced what happened when I was driving in Bari, surrounded by people whose stubbornness is as second nature to them as breathing is to the rest of us.

At first glance Bari looks no worse than any other ancient city forced to deal with the realities of a modern world. Streets are narrow. Some go around in circles. They cross at weird angles. They end abruptly at fences and walls. They are rarely smoothly paved. Conflicting and confusing signs abound. All this is bad enough. But the drivers, they are incredible.

Every car ride is an adventure. The stop signs, the streetlights, the one-way signs mean absolutely nothing. A shrug of the shoulders translates, "Idiot! You should have known why I made the decision to go this way, so get out of my way." Double-parking is not the norm; triple-parking, with blinkers flashing, is what everyone does. This leads to irate drivers getting out of their Fiats and Opels because the street is blocked to scream at cars with nobody in them until their owners come out of a store and start yelling back. At this point everyone else who is blocked starts honking, and then they get out of their cars and start arguing about who is responsible for the initial violation.

To stop and ask directions, map in hand, is to invite disaster. The person you ask immediately draws another stranger into the discussion. They soon forget not only that you are standing there but also what it was that started their present argument. Too many times I have muttered, "Grazi" and left without my map, more confused than when I stopped, leaving my "helpers" to their heated debate.

Perhaps because there are so many monuments and circular streets, I always seemed to get where I wanted to go. More often than not, I had absolutely no idea how I got there. But almost magically the train station, the hotel, the cathedral, or the restaurant would appear. I'd look at the map and realize that I had reached my destination without even beginning to follow the directions so carefully highlighted for me. I could relax for a while until I started thinking about how I was going to get back.

It is easy to find parallels between driving in Bari and dealing with God's will. In life, we carefully map our route and plan what we want to do and how we are going to do it. But God's will for us may not always match our plans and desires. In our stubbornness we plod onward, certain that what we want is what is best for us. So when we are finally good and lost, we turn to God and ask for help—when we could have simply been open to God's direction to begin with. We fail to trust that God will always be with us. We forget that our prayer should be, "Your will be done."

Like Jonah, who went west when God wanted him to go east to Nineveh, we stubbornly go the direction of our own choosing. But just like Jonah, spit out of a whale onto the shore of Nineveh, we end up, after all our maneuvering around, exactly where God wanted us all along. And for some reason we are surprised. We folks from Bari aren't the only ones with the hard heads, are we?

Stories of God's Love

No gift is more freely given to us than God's love. Perhaps that is why we take it for granted and too often fail to feel its power, its peace, and its healing. Many of us are blessed with parents who have mingled God's love with their own love for us, making for a powerful and wondrous combination. We can

> "I give you a new commandment: love one another; just as I have loved you, you also must love one another. By this love you have for one another, everyone will know that you are my disciples."

~ JOHN 13:34–35

---

also know the blessing of finding God's love in other very special people. We are most aware of what this love means to us when, for whatever reason, it is kept from us, which is all the more reason for becoming conduits of that love ourselves.

mrs. la france

ONE LADY FROM MY CHILDHOOD STANDS OUT AS definitely out of the ordinary. She was one of those people who mystify us long after they're gone. Whether they know it or not, they touch us even years later.

My mother met her one Sunday on the crowded front steps of the church after Mass. They probably just bumped into one another. In those days, the crowd would pour out into the street, stopping traffic and leaving the organist blasting out a postlude on the gigantic Aeolian Skinner.

We would never really know where this woman came from. But all of a sudden there she was one sunny afternoon, sitting at our kitchen table (the heart and soul of our house), enjoying a bowl of freshly cooked pasta and regaling my mother with stories of sophisticated living in New York City. This would be the first of many such visits. My mother was always a good audience. The woman's tales were long, with enough colorful details to get her through two or three bowls of steaming rigatoni before she would sigh contentedly, look at the clock on the wall, and tell us that she had to be on her way.

She was always impeccably dressed in an old-fashioned sort of way. I think of her when I watch reruns of old TV shows like *I Love Lucy*. Even in the summer she was never without a feathered hat perched dramatically on her head, and a swath of red lipstick blended with Mom's tomato sauce in a bold arch across her lips.

She spoke with an accent that my mother, who was no stranger to accents, quickly labeled "continental," whatever that meant. And with the exotic name of "Mrs. La France," she became an intriguing character for my brothers and me, probably because we were as far from continental as you could get and still be in the same species.

We looked forward to her visits and would sit without fighting and listen to her stories in genuine awe. Her tales were filled with much personal advice to each of us boys in the form of little asides—how to dress better or comb our hair or clean our nails. She would talk about faraway places as though she'd visited them.

We decided that she must have been a teacher once upon a time. And we would watch in amazement as our petite Mrs. La France would pack away pasta, oxtails, bread, salad, and red wine spritzed with ginger ale. But she was unfailingly well mannered. When one of my brothers asked her, with intense seriousness, the proper end from which to bite into a celery stalk, she offered him the most sensible answer: whichever end reaches your lips first. We decided that we liked her, and she would always smile and say hello to us when we saw her on the street.

One day, with the pasta boiling well beyond al dente, Mrs. La France missed her appointed arrival at our house, which was very unlike her. She had no telephone; it was, she said, a nuisance and a rude interruption. But Mom had her address. And so, worried that Mrs. La France might be ill, Mom sent one of my older brothers to her apartment with a huge pot of chicken soup, fresh bread, and some fruit.

My brother's return was surprisingly quick. He informed us that Mrs. La France's apartment was little more than one small room in a run-down boardinghouse. Mrs. La France was indeed sick but also very angry that her privacy had been invaded. She told my poor brother to tell my mother to leave her alone and that we should all just let her be. She did take all the food, however.

We didn't see Mrs. La France after that, not at church or even on the street. I have a feeling that Mom knew she would never appear on our doorstep again. Blame it on embarrassment or stubbornness or pride, but Mrs. La France would forever shut us out for having invaded her circle of privacy and perhaps for having found out more than she wanted us to know about her.

We could tell that for a long time Mom felt bad about what had happened. She sent Mrs. La France a birthday card and later a Christmas card, but there was never any response. Mom had to patiently explain to my brothers and me why Mrs. La France had grown angry with us. Young as we were, we really weren't able to understand. But Mom made sure we didn't feel guilty about trying to be good neighbors.

A year or so passed. Then, on an afternoon I remember so clearly, I saw Mom putting on her good coat. There were tears in her eyes. The newspaper was open to the obituaries. Mom had circled the name "La France." She went out quietly. When she came home from the wake a few hours later, all she told us was that, while she was there, no one else came to say a prayer or to mourn Mrs. La France's passing.

"I hope we made her happy for a little while, at least," Mom said. Then she walked quietly into the kitchen to fix our dinner.

God's love is freely given to us. And, like most of God's gifts, it comes from many and varied sources. We can choose—in our pride or fear or hurt—to reject that love. Or we can humbly and joyfully accept it. It will never run out. Even better, God will continue to offer it even after we've rejected it time and time again.

God's love is unconditional. And God already knows the true condition of our lives. So we have no need to be ashamed or to hide from God's efforts to help and love us.

a father's son

I USED TO WATCH IN AWE AS MY FATHER CAME
out of the back room of the family grocery store with
a hundred-pound sack of Idaho potatoes slung over
his shoulder. His red face gave away how strenuous
the job was. But without missing a stride he would
carry it up the aisle to the produce department and
with one swift motion toss it dramatically onto the
bin. I was both proud and scared of his strength.

Dad enjoyed hard work. In the store, he was
usually smiling or whistling to himself. He never took
a break. He was always finding something to do. I
guess that since he was shy he enjoyed the solitary,
physical aspects of the job. It was easier than having to
deal with the customers and their complaints or with
the family when he returned home late in the day.

Looking back now, I realize how quickly the
years passed. I grew up. I entered the seminary. In

my father's eyes I wasn't a man until I was ordained and had become self-sufficient. Yet, how incredibly different my life was from my father's. I was a parish priest, and he was a sturdy, hardworking grocer.

My own life grew so busy that I barely noticed my father growing older. He began taking an occasional long lunch away from the store. Then it was a half day off. That led to his taking a day or two to rest from his growing aches and pains. One afternoon, without warning, he decided to retire. He left the business to his brother—a real surprise to my brothers, to say the least—and that was that. He never talked about his retirement or about anything of much substance relating to his life. I wish now that I had asked him how he felt at crucial times. But he was a man of few words and seldom shared his feelings.

As more years passed, his health began to fail. It's sad how easily we block out what we don't want to see. My father and I both denied what was happening to him. So how ironic it was that, late in life and in spite of himself, my father taught me a lesson in how it feels to grow old.

It was well past dark on a frigid Sunday. I was leaving my parents' home for the rectory when my car got stuck in the snow in the alley behind the house. I was hoping Dad wouldn't hear my tires spinning. But I should have known he would. He always watched from the kitchen window until I pulled away. And so in the midst of my frustrated muttering, I saw him coming out of the house with a pitchfork, of all things, to help me get my car out of the ruts.

No doubt Dad's hearing was fine, but his weak eyes worried me. I feared that the sharp pitchfork would puncture one of my tires. But of much greater concern was my dad's heart, which was nowhere near as young as it used to be. I didn't want him to overexert himself. At that sad moment I realized that a fragile old man, red in the face and short of breath, had somehow replaced the strong, silently powerful father of my youth.

I asked him to stop trying to help me, but he refused to listen, his face showing the sweat from the strain. What else could I do? I grabbed the pitchfork from him and surprised myself, loudly ordering him back into the house. He gave me a long, hard look and then, cursing, slowly retreated to the kitchen. Neighbors had heard the noise and were coming out to give me the push I needed to get unstuck.

I felt lousy as I drove off, thinking that Dad must really be angry with me. As soon as I got back to the rectory I called home. Mom answered and confirmed that Dad was angry all right, but not at me. He was angry with himself for growing old and not being able to help his son as he felt a father should, for not being able to do those things he had once been capable of doing. It was a sad moment for us all.

Dad was with us for only a few years after that night. During that time I grew much more conscious of his battle with growing old. I watched closely but helplessly as he fought dying even to his last days.

I especially feel his loss when holidays like Father's Day come around. I must face his absence again and again. But in some way I want him to know how much I loved him that night in the cold and the snow—and that I still love him.

Now, as I watch myself grow older, I realize that the father I'll always remember is the strong, proud, hardworking father of my youth. While my work does not entail lifting hundred-pound sacks of potatoes, and while as a priest I'll never have children of my own to rescue, pitchfork in hand, from some icy alley, I am grateful. Maybe it's because I am starting to see a lot of him in me and I am grateful to him for that.

We are taught that we are made in God's image. In some strange way, we are God's children. We speak of God as Father or Mother, as protector and provider. Yet we are separate and different from the heavenly Parent, and we will never completely understand that love, so freely and tenaciously given to us. We can, however, trust that the perfect love of God will be reproduced in us. It will appear in our lives because it has become part of us. As we mature, that love will come shining through.

a mother's gift

century, no one knew what to call the sickness. A
child suffering from it would be pale and sickly from
birth and, growing weaker with each passing year,
would probably not survive until adulthood.

Today someone with this condition is diag-
nosed as having a "chronic" strain of Mediterranean
anemia, or if they die, it is considered the "perni-
cious" variety. Back then, not much could be done. A
child who was lucky would be sent to the farm of a
relative or friend, where it was hoped that the fresh
eggs and meats and clean country air would bring
about a cure. This is what happened to my mother
when she was a young child.

Fortunately the cure worked very well, as my
mother, approaching her ninth decade in good
health and spirits, can attest. What's interesting is
that, besides healing her physically, those years in

the country turned out to be perhaps her most formative years in other ways. During that time she learned much that would stay with her, helping her become the vital and interesting person she is now.

It was there that she learned all the wonderful peasant recipes that are at once simple and complex. Her *polpettas*—fried egg balls—rank with the finest dishes. The style is called "contadina," and its subtleties are rarely found in restaurants in this country.

She also learned the rustic wisdom shared through legends about the saints and in folktales and proverbs that were told around the hearth late at night. And while she listened, she learned how to crochet such fine pieces that, many years later, department stores offered to buy her work on consignment.

She went from the farm in Italy to a shoe factory in upstate New York, where she worked for years doing piecework at a sewing machine. The toll that took on her, in the form of arthritis, has made such intricate sewing nearly impossible for her today. But she still delights in knitting afghans and blankets in wonderfully tight patterns. Everyone in the family has one or more. She has completed special ones for every grandchild. And she is working on blankets for her great-grandchildren, including some who aren't even born—to be saved, she says, in case "I am no longer around when they are baptized."

Each year she finishes an afghan for my parish's silent auction. It is guaranteed to earn a high bid, partly because she insists that I advertise it as the last one she will ever make. But each year she ends up making another one as beautiful as the rest.

I look at my brothers and their wives and their grown children with their own spouses, and I see the impact my mother has made on the family. She continues to be a genuine grace for us. It goes well beyond recipes and sewing techniques. She has shared her wisdom with us as well, along with an attitude that constantly challenges us to be strong, good people.

So I am not at all surprised when I hear about my brothers' children bringing their boyfriends or girlfriends to Mom, not only for her approval, but also that she might share her insights and stories with them. I am also proud that so many people in her retirement complex come and talk with her when they are feeling down or alone. Her common-sense approach to life is just what they need. And when I hear about Mom leading the seniors from her building into the kitchen en masse to protest the declining quality of the food, threatening to lead them all in a boycott, I smile and realize that the apple hasn't fallen far from the tree. When I see how animated she becomes and how the years just fade from her face as she shares a story or a reflection from her rich life, I know at that moment that she has given me more than I realize. I am proud that she says I take after her.

Imitation is the highest form of flattery. To be like someone who has given us so much is to pay her or him the utmost compliment. God's love makes us more than we could ever be on our own. That love is as much our heritage as is the mother's or father's or grandparent's love that has shaped us. What a wonderful gift we can give to the world—to imitate God's love too.

tough lover

GOD'S LOVE IS A TOUGH LOVE. GOD MAKES
incredible demands on us, the premier challenge
being to love one another as God has chosen to love
us. It is so tough, in fact, that I am convinced that
most of us turn away from it, run from it, and misin-
terpret it. It is no wonder, then, that those who try
to love as God loves—those courageous heroes—are
the ones who often find themselves vilified, excom-
municated, burnt at the stake. Only after they are
gone is their powerful love at a safe enough distance
for them to be sanctified by the very ones who
attacked them.

Maureen is one of those tough lovers. In her
mind, compromise ultimately dilutes the challenging
but simple gospel edict to love as Jesus loved. That
love is marked by the sign of his cross.

Maureen could have led an unremarkable life.
She could have chosen to stay in her cozy suburban

home with her quiet, supportive, and patient husband and their children, a home where the front door has never been locked. She could have found a part-time job as a social worker to keep her busy, adding a little income to the family coffers and helping her feel good about herself.

Instead, she and a visionary priest founded a program to deal with the explosion of teen pregnancies in her solidly conservative Catholic suburb. The parish-based program, aptly named Courage, quickly became a resource of last resort for frightened children and desperate parents. Maureen and her dedicated group of volunteers were good at what they did. Some would insist that they were too good.

Tough love requires that we be proactive. It wasn't enough for Maureen and Courage to be satisfied sitting back answering calls and directing families to available resources. Something much more radical needed to be done to keep decent but frantic people from choosing abortion because they could not see any other viable options. No matter how many resources Courage was able to provide, the larger battle was still being lost.

So Maureen and Courage moved into prevention, opening up offices at local Catholic high schools and giving talks and presentations to anyone who was willing to listen, from parents' groups to religious classes, CCD teachers, and young-adult gatherings. She mixed facts with firsthand accounts and a challenge to love and get involved.

A loving response does not soften the message, sugarcoat the delivery, or please its audience with pious niceties and words they want to hear. Tough love often opposes the status quo. This is frequently Maureen's position. "Not here," "Not in this neighborhood," and "Not our children" are the responses of people who are unwilling to face a desperate reality. She hears such phrases from those whose political agendas have made them self-righteous protectors of a morality that exists only in their imaginations. When people don't like the message, they blame the messenger. Maureen has been criticized for being too blunt, too shocking, too impatient, too challenging. If only she could tone down her anger, clean up her vocabulary, and be a little bit more submissive to the authorities.

As her clients have grown in number to the thousands Maureen's loving response has not suited some of her hearers. Her clear message of abstinence is based on reality, a reality made more frightening by the growing spectrum of life-threatening sexually transmitted diseases. Her forceful message "Don't" also includes a loving plea not to compound the mistake by being ignorant and going unprotected. For this, her orthodoxy is challenged regularly.

How sadly ironic that someone who loves so deeply and works so hard to protect countless unborn babies and their troubled young mothers (and fathers) is constantly being "called onto the carpet" by numerous officials. Equally sad is how quickly the support—even from those she helps—fades under the heat of outside criticism.

Yet Maureen has never wavered. People leaflet her. Sometimes frightened pastors withdraw their invitations, unwilling to take the heat publicly for something they claim to support privately. She has been labeled "a loose cannon" and "impossible to work with."

But Maureen and Courage continue. Her love attracts volunteers who are unafraid. Through it all, she finds the time and energy to support good people who are performing loving ministries of all sorts. She meets and prays regularly with seniors. She has started a support group for women active in ministry.

Maureen laughs at the pompous responses she elicits. She cries when injustice burdens faith-filled people trying to live the gospel. Her love is not based on rhetoric, but her loving response is invariably challenging. And Courage keeps on being there for those who have nowhere else to turn.

All of us want to experience God's love in our hearts. But are we willing to be challenged by it, to be made uncomfortable, and ultimately to be misunderstood for embracing it? God's love, and the messages it generates, can be troubling.

not in my
neighborhood

IT HAS BEEN A PROTRACTED BATTLE WITH MORE
moves than a chess match between champions.
There have been moments filled with despair, and
there have been flashes of ecstasy. It has become a
cause. Like crusaders from all over Europe gathering
to recapture the Holy Land, clergy, community orga-
nizations, and people of goodwill have come together to support a neighboring parish. The parish
wants to turn its empty forty-five-room convent into
a transitional housing program sponsored by one of
the most respected religious agencies in the city.

Initially the proposal took on a David-versus-
Goliath appearance. Opposition came from a local
neighborhood organization armed with lawyers, developers, and well-connected officers. Their not-so-
hidden agenda was simple: "Not in my neighborhood."
They set the rules for the initial referendum and then

changed the bylaws and membership regulations as to who could vote. The alderman said he would support whatever the vote indicated. At an emotional meeting, it was voted down by a narrow margin.

The pastor and his parishioners were stunned not only by the lack of freedom to do with their property what they felt was a legitimate continuation of the parish's history and mission but also by the viciousness of the opposition. Zoning inspectors suddenly appeared at the parish, writing up violations. Developers arrogantly offered over a million dollars for the property. These developers apparently had direct lines to the officers of the neighborhood organization who were at that time writing the pastor's provincial, demanding his termination.

When I and other priests, ministers, and rabbis found this out we gathered in support of the pastor and the housing proposal. When I met with the alderman, he threw down the gauntlet by asking if we had the stomach for a protracted battle. We did. We set up meetings and held press conferences. A candlelight vigil took place. The media began reporting our story. We visited neighbors, polling them and giving them accurate information. Petitions were distributed and signed. Additional meetings with the opposition were held separately and together at the alderman's office. Accusations flew in both directions. A neophyte in the political arena, I often questioned my own effectiveness in the whole process.

As of this writing, the tide of the battle has turned, and support for the deserving project led to its unanimous approval by the Zoning Board of Appeals.

One particular night in the midst of all this, I came home to the rectory quite late. I had canceled all of my evening appointments to attend a planning meeting and two other meetings at the alderman's office, one with a large group of supporters and the others to talk face-to-face in a smaller group setting with the opponents of the proposal. I was tired and I was confused. But I knew for sure that helping the homeless return to permanent housing was right and just.

But there on the front steps of the rectory, sound asleep and blocking the entrance, was a homeless person wrapped in a piece of tattered carpeting. His beer can was empty and his bottle of port open, in easy reach for him to take a swig as soon as he awakened.

Anger flashed in me. I was all for housing the homeless, but not on my front steps at that time of night. With no other way of entering the rectory, I was forced to wake him. It wasn't easy. The beer and wine had done their job too well. When he finally stirred into consciousness, I told him he had to move and stop blocking the entrance to the rectory. He moved slowly enough that I decided he was deliberately trying to anger me further.

I finally just stepped over him and pushed my way into the rectory. After checking my messages, I looked out the door to see if he had moved on.

I must have really made him angry. He had finished the wine and tossed the bottle, breaking it against the rectory door. I then watched as he proceeded to urinate all over the steps. I waited behind the door until he was finished and then began to sputter and yell that I was going to call the police. Looking satisfied, he loped away.

Hearing my own angry shouts, I suddenly realized that I was no better than the opponents of the housing for the homeless. Like them, I was thinking, *Not in my neighborhood.* But the wet doorstep and the pieces of glass kept my anger alive. The best I could do was shout after him, "God loves you, man, fortunately a lot more than I do at this moment."

How easy it is for me, and for a lot of us, to love our neighbors when they are far enough away from us that our path is not blocked and we are not offended by their smell. How easy it is when they are grateful and respond on our terms. How easy it is to get behind a cause and forget the human person right there in front of us.

We should be grateful that God doesn't love that way. God takes us for who we are and where we are, no matter what we are doing. And then God challenges us to love each other in the same way. Sometimes that is the hardest battle of all.

Stories of God's Grace

For me, God's grace is like sunlight reflecting on a pond that is stirred by a soft breeze. Grace is beautiful, fragile, gentle, and even playful. Where it comes from and why it comes to me, I don't know. But it becomes part of who I am, giving me memories of

> "Be compassionate as your Father is compassionate. Do not judge, and you will not be judged yourselves; do not condemn, and you will not be condemned yourselves; grant pardon, and you will be pardoned. Give, and there will be gifts for you: a full measure, pressed down, shaken together, and running over, will be poured into your lap; because the amount you measure out is the amount you will be given back."
>
> ~ LUKE 6:36–38

cooks and plumbers,

of vacations and visits to nursing homes. I've had a life full of watching that grace reflected in so many other lives. I've watched firsthand as it made an incredible difference to the people who were open to it.

ode to a short-order cook

ON THE CORNER JUST WEST OF OUR LADY OF
Mount Carmel school and church was a Rexall drugstore. For any kid with an imagination (as if that
doesn't define what a kid is), this store was a great
place to explore. On its shelves were the magical
cures for just about whatever disease or ailment
could strike the human body. On other shelves, gathering dust, were all sorts of things for which, with a
little creativity, you could find new and different
uses. A screw-top pillbox, for example, became a
great container for the lead sinkers I needed on my
bamboo fishing pole. And a pumice stone was perfect
for keeping my forbidden penknife razor sharp. But
let me stop giving away all my youthful secrets.

Besides all those mysterious and wonderful
contraptions and elixirs, there was a candy counter
of monumental proportions. There you could find
Turkish Taffy and Zagnut bars alongside Forever

Yours and Smith Brothers wild cherry cough drops. The choices were practically endless.

There also was a lunch counter and four or five booths tucked away in the back corner of the store. At noon on any weekday you could find fifteen to twenty-five customers enjoying a hamburger or the meat-loaf special or a couple of eggs over easy. It was there one fateful morning that I developed my lifelong love of grits, having been bribed by a classmate who was born and raised in Memphis.

The memorable thing about that lunch counter was that, while there were always two or three waitresses on duty, there was only one short-order cook, and he handled every order. And it was the same person there all day, every day. I would watch him closely as I drank my chocolate phosphate.

I was mesmerized by the energy and economy of motion as this cook worked the grill, the toaster, the burners, and the coolers. No matter how busy he was, he displayed this intensity and a sense of confident organization. He was in control at all times. To a klutzy ten-year-old he was a marvel to watch.

A child is not good at determining an adult's age. I guessed that he was middle-aged, whatever that meant to me back then. I remember thinking that his clothes looked older, almost dated, even in those days. His pleated pants and suspenders and white rolled-up sleeves probably made him appear older than his years. Bespectacled, short, and wiry, he could have been a flyweight boxer earlier in life.

To my surprise and delight, I noticed that he was attending daily Mass at the church—the early Mass at six-thirty in the morning. This was the one that Sister always seemed to give my brothers and me to serve, which might have been because we lived fairly close to the church. More than likely it was because our mother always made sure that we were up and on time for our assignments.

No matter how long before Mass I would arrive to serve, the cook was already there in church. And no matter how long I stuck around, he'd remain longer, caught up in devout prayer. He wore a tie and a suit coat over that white work shirt, and he would turn in his daily missal from one ribboned section to the next with the same compact energy he would later use to chop up a pickle and garnish five sandwiches.

All this impressed me. And, young as I was, I realized that he couldn't be earning a great salary as a short-order cook. But there was no way of tipping him, as when I left the waitress a dime.

It sounds awfully silly now, but I decided that I had to somehow let him know that I appreciated how hard he worked. The holidays were approaching, and I determined to buy him a gift. I couldn't give it to him while he was working, so I decided to present it to him after Mass some morning before Christmas.

I found the perfect gift. When no one was looking I took a really neat chef's hat from a Del Monte display in my family's grocery store. I put it in a new-looking Sears box I found in my grandmother's closet. Then I wrapped it all up with shiny Christmas paper.

I waited until a day or so before Christmas and then ran up and handed it to him, leaving him with a quizzical look on his face as he walked toward the Rexall store.

For days I peeked from around the candy counter hoping I'd see him wearing the chef's hat. But it never was on his head. Once on the weekend, I even tried to sneak behind the counter to see if I could locate the box. But I never found anything at all. For a long time I consoled myself by thinking that he must have liked it so much that he didn't want to get it dirty or sweaty. Perhaps he had placed it on his mantel at home, as if it were some kind of Oscar or Emmy for cooks.

I can't pinpoint when I stopped watching him deep in prayer in the pew or when other people replaced him in my interest. But after a lot of years I am still grateful that he showed me a little about hard work and even harder prayer. And I hope that the ten-year-old I was then brought him a little bit of satisfaction and maybe even some joy. I guess I'll never know. But that's okay.

God's grace, so freely given to us, sometimes arrives in strange packages—a challenge, an illness, an opportunity, a new start, a broken relationship. It appears in the form of regular folks who work hard and pray hard. Maybe it even makes itself known in the children who look up to those folks. The short-order cook gave me the gift of his example, and the gift of my admiration was worthy too. We never know how our simple yet noble responses become reflections of God, to whom they are ultimately directed.

the
pilgrimage

AS DAD GREW OLDER AND REALIZED THAT HE
would never travel back to Italy again, he made Mom
promise that she would take the whole family to
Italy after he died, to visit the hometown. She kept
her promise. All of us, including spouses and children, numbered thirteen and spanned more than
seven decades. If even one of us couldn't have made
it, the trip would not have happened. It took a year
of planning to pull it together.

As fate would have it, my appointment as pastor came down less than a week before we were
scheduled to leave. I remember telling the priest per-
sonnel board that they could name me pope, but it
would have to wait. I wasn't going to let anything
get in the way of that trip.

From the moment we left, our travels took on
the mystical feel of a pilgrimage. The eight-hour
delay on the tarmac in the rain at JFK Airport should

have alerted us that this would be a once-in-a-life-time experience.

There were so many unforgettable moments. There was the ridiculous $850 dinner at the outdoor café in the Piazza Minerva in Rome. There was also that indescribable feeling when we reached the tiny church in Corregio, the village where my father was born. In the church we found a marble plaque thanking him and my uncles for the money they sent from America to build that simple little house of God. There I celebrated Mass in my halting Italian with a priest so short I kept checking to see if I was standing on the wrong stair. The whole village came out for that Mass to see the Americans. The young men were much more interested in my blonde nieces.

There were many moments of laughter, but none so sustained as when we, along with other tourists, were quietly admiring a wall of Rembrandt paintings in Florence—and somebody passed gas. My mother, who was not the culprit, shouted, "Don't look at me!" and we broke into such loud laughter that guards came running in from other rooms to see what was going on.

Other moments were so sublime that there was nothing to say. When I saw the five-hundred-year-old olive tree in the center of the family farm still run by my uncle, I could only sit under it and imagine my father as a child on the same spot, dreaming of coming to America for a new life. I thought of what hope and courage must have existed in him even then. And when I walked into the small backyard of the house where my mother was born, I saw what had to be hundreds of fragrant blooming rose bushes. Then I understood why roses are still so special to my mother.

There were beautiful, life-sustaining memories, moments of grace. When we finally arrived at the cathedral in Alberobello, the hometown and our final destination, we instinctively spread out to be alone with our prayers and thoughts. Throughout our growing-up years we had seen pictures of the statues of the patron saints Cosmas and Damian, who were early martyrs from Asia Minor. Now those gilded statues were before us.

Mom came up to each one of us and grabbed us by the hand. She had waited and prepared for this time to share something personal and private with each one of us. At that moment our common heritage and the roots of our faith bonded us as a family in a way that continues to stay with us. Over the three weeks that we traveled throughout Italy, we saw the magnificent cathedrals in Milan and Florence. We were struck by the beauty and splendor of St. Peter's Basilica and the rest of the Vatican. We stood before the bones of Saint Peter. We visited the beautiful and simple birthplace of Pope John XXIII.

We explored the caverns of Casteliano. But nothing left the life-shaping imprint of those few moments in the hometown cathedral.

A pilgrimage is supposed to be a journey that helps us get in touch with the core of our faith so that it can be nurtured and grow stronger. Dad's dying gift to us and Mom's kept promise helped our family appreciate the origins of our belief in a loving and protecting God. And we learned a little more about why we are the way we are. We owe our renewed sense of family and faith to those moments in the hometown church and to the journey that brought us there.

All of the other feelings and memories we brought home with us were wonderful bonuses. We will remember the look on my nieces' faces when they found out they were eating the rabbit they had been playing with the day before. We will hold dear those moments when we greeted relatives we had never seen before. This pilgrimage led us not only home but also into the depths of our souls. We will carry this knowledge with us wherever our lives take us.

There will be times in our lives when we feel that we are alone—when we are in the desert. But thank God for the times when we realize how rich and incredibly graced our lives are and how blessed we've become. We need to store those special, lush remembrances so that we can draw on them when we are parched and dry. It takes time and effort to recognize, understand, and internalize God's grace. Pilgrimage costs us. But, as we find new resources within us when we need them most, we know that the price was quite reasonable.

dreams
and grace

HIS ACCENT WAS AS GERMAN AS HIS NAME: Hans. I met him one Saturday while bringing the Eucharist to residents of the local nursing home. A nurse pointed Hans out to me, telling me that, although he wasn't Catholic, he wanted very much to talk to a priest. I looked over at him and saw a feeble old man, hunched over and in some pain. I figured that he was lonely and saw in me the opportunity to talk with someone. Reluctantly I introduced myself and at that moment met one of the most fascinating people I will ever be privileged to know.

Hans, in his early sixties, was actually younger than he looked. But he was ravaged by spinal cancer, along with the side effects of the morphine necessary to alleviate the worst of his pain. He spoke slowly, as though he had carefully considered every word. At that first encounter, he informed me that he wanted to convert to Catholicism before his death. Would I give him instructions in the faith? I assured him I would visit him regularly, but I still suspected that he might merely be hooking me into filling some time for him.

The next time I visited Hans he was in his room. It was a wonderful collage of his entire life. He had been an engineer before illness struck. His wife was deceased, but he had a number of children, who visited him regularly. As a youth he had been conscripted into the army of the Third Reich but within two weeks had been captured by advancing Soviet troops. He'd spent years in a concentration camp in Siberia. He could hypnotize you with his stories.

I asked him why he wanted to become a Catholic. He said that his maternal grandmother had been a Catholic. His earliest memory was of being lifted up in her arms to see out a window. There, a golden sun rose over a deep blue lake with mist rising from it. And she said to him, "Look, look, drink in the beauty and never forget that there is a God who loves you." This moment had become a recurring dream for him. It was the impetus behind his desire to convert.

We met often to talk. Despite all the tragedy and pain in his life, Hans continually searched for beauty. Once, from the clutter of a messy desk he brought out a small coin. It was a Roman coin used in Galilee around the time Jesus had lived. Hans was completely in awe of it, realizing that there was a possibility, however remote, that Jesus had touched the coin that now rested reverently in his hand. Hans would leave this coin to his oldest child.

A seminarian intern lived at our parish at that time. As much as I enjoyed Hans's company, I felt it was a superb opportunity to give this student the gift of Hans's dream. So I had the young person who was just beginning his life's work prepare this dying man to enter the Catholic Church. The seminarian often came home in awe of what Hans had shared with him. They journeyed together over a landscape of dreams. Finally, Hans made the first of only two trips into our church. That day he was baptized and received the Eucharist for the first time, tears streaming down his face, his family present, the congregation applauding. It made for a graced Sunday liturgy.

The seminarian left to complete his studies, and I continued to bring Hans the Eucharist and to be fed by his dreams. Hans died a year later, and his body was brought to the church for the second and final time. I was never more reverent with the holy water and the incense. I would miss Hans.

Hans's life was touched early on by God's grace. No one knew it would take an entire lifetime before that grace manifested itself to Hans. And when that time came, many of us were blessed to share in God's special gift to this long-searching son.

Wouldn't it be good if each of us found a Hans? So many dreams could be shared, and we could learn so much. After all, don't we all need to see how close we can come to touching Jesus, as Hans did with that Roman coin? And don't we all need someone's enduring and final dream to keep us dreaming—or to get us started dreaming once again?

Look around at the people in, or at the edge of, your life. You never know who lives in your home, in your neighbor's home, or in that imposing institution down the street. Until you meet people and talk with them, you'll never know the dreams they own and how those dreams might touch you. I believe that, somewhere, there is a Hans who would enjoy nothing more than to share with you his story and, perhaps, the grace of his last dream.

christmas morning music

NOTHING REPRESENTS GOD'S GRACE FREELY
given to us better than Christmas. Dad taught this to
my brothers and me many years ago.

Louie was a butcher who worked for Dad in
our family grocery store. When I was a young child it
never occurred to me that people actually worked for
my father and uncle. They seemed more like part of
our extended family. To a person they all tolerated
my brothers and me. Perhaps it was because we were
the boss's children, or maybe it was because my
family always treated them with respect and dignity
and generosity. Many times they would come to
our house for a Sunday cookout or a homemade
pasta dinner, which my mother would prepare
with gusto. Everyone was welcome.

Louie came to our home on the same day each
year. His visit was on Christmas morning, precisely at
the time we were getting ready to gather as a family

to open our presents. The festively wrapped gifts called to us from under the tree in the dining-room alcove. The tree itself was usually the scrawniest, ugliest one you could imagine because Dad would always bring home one that he knew he wouldn't be able to sell. But that's a different story altogether.

When Louie inevitably arrived, dressed nattily in his overcoat, his fedora tilted rakishly to one side and his gray, pencil-thin mustache perfectly trimmed, he actually looked more like a five-foot-five-inch banker than the white-smocked, blood-splattered butcher I was used to seeing in the store. Dad would usher my brothers and me past the presents under the tree to the living-room couch where we would sit four across, with a good deal of poking and elbowing until one of Dad's patented looks stopped us instantly.

When Louie made his appearance each year, he brought along a tattered violin case. His gift to us was to be a melody or two played on his old wooden fiddle. Dad would introduce this event to us four boys with great flourish.

Louie would begin by gently lifting the violin out of its case as though it were a delicate antique. Then it would take him a good quarter hour of precious Christmas-morning time to caress the polished wood with a dusting cloth and begin the process of tuning it one string at a time.

The problem was that, in all the years of my childhood, Louie never made it beyond this step. Either a string turned up broken (I guessed that it was the same string three years in a row) or Louie had inexplicably but most apologetically forgotten the bow. (That excuse worked for a couple of years.) More apologies would follow until Dad slapped him on the back with good humor and assured him that all was fine. If he couldn't play anything on the violin, perhaps he could honor us by singing a classic Italian aria. Dad would boast to us that Louie had been in the chorus at La Scala in Milan. Each year Dad would tell us this, and each year we'd nod, dutifully impressed but without a clue as to what he meant.

Louie would give us a stiff little bow and ask for a small glass of water for his throat, then for a little anisette, and then for a little more anisette. Then he'd make some strange guttural sounds and sadly shake his head. No, he would tell us, his voice was just not in proper shape for him to sing for us (despite the pint or so of anisette he had drunk to aid it). More apologies.

Dad would tell him to never mind. We would be happy to wait until next Christmas. Louie, now looking much relieved, would have a cup of espresso and a few biscotti before putting on his coat. With a crisp tip of his hat, he would wish us all "buon natale" and be off.

I don't think we were supposed to see Dad slipping Louie a fifty-dollar bill as he walked out the door, but we did. No matter, our attention was quickly diverted. With this annual tradition finally taken care of, my brothers and I would run to the Christmas tree to open our presents. Mom would pause from her cooking, Dad would sit down with a self-satisfied grin, and we'd begin.

I realize now that Louie probably could not play a note on the violin if his life depended on it. I am equally certain that he never sang an aria, even in the shower. But it didn't matter at all.

The presents under the tree were always exciting to open and to play with. If the grocery store had had a good year, there would be a few more. Almost a half-century later I cannot tell you what those presents were. But I will never forget the simple gift Dad gave my brothers and me as, each Christmas, we witnessed his generosity to Louie, the violin-playing, aria-singing butcher.

We don't need to earn God's grace by performance or talent. God gives it to us freely, all the time treating us like family and preserving our dignity. Once we have received it from God, how will we choose to share the gift?

anniversary reflections

TWENTY-FIVE YEARS AGO, ALMOST FORTY OF US knelt nervously in the sanctuary of the seminary's main chapel during the rite of ordination. At one point in the ceremony, as a sign of solidarity with us, priests of the archdiocese came forward and laid their hands on our heads. Among these priests we were a very popular class. Some classmates, like me, had the long hair and bushy sideburns that reflected those early seventies values of pushing the limits. Others were more traditional and steadfast in appearance and attitude. Our diversity in outlook and, more important, our common burning desire to serve, united us as a class and made us well liked by others.

It was the beginning of an end of an era. But we did not know it then. The laying on of hands took so long, with so many priests, that the powers that be had to politely stop the process after the first six hundred had come past us. Not only that, but because we were a large class, some of us had to kneel on a bare marble floor rather than on a padded Oriental carpet. In anticipation of this, we unlucky ones were given kneepads to wear discreetly under our vestments. However, some priests, in the intensity of their laying on of hands, pressed down on our heads so hard that I was constantly doing the kneeling splits on the slippery marble. I had to keep scooting up. By the time this portion of the ceremony was over I was exhausted and sore.

After we processed out of the chapel and posed for the traditional class picture on the front steps, we stationed ourselves around the main circle of the campus to give our first blessings to family, friends, and strangers. At one point, I remember pausing and looking at my classmates, so clerical in their black suits. Their intensity shocked me. I wondered if I looked like that. I'm sure now that I did.

Little did any of us know that for at least the next twenty-five years people, events, and circumstances would continue to press down on our heads. God's grace would be not only the burden we were called to shoulder but also the power that would lift us up.

Over the years, some among us would feel the burden more powerfully than the grace and would leave active ministry. The reasons for this vary as much as our distinct and individual appearances of that first day. Some left, feeling that they had not fully realized how demanding it would be. Some felt the heavy burden of celibacy. Addictions of various sorts made it impossible for some to continue. Others seemed to simply fade away.

Sadly, death would capture too early some of the brightest, most creative, and liveliest among us. It was almost as though they had spent their allotted portion of living faster than the rest of us. Ironically, they were the ones with whom I would have wanted to grow old.

On that day a quarter of a century ago, our dreams were vivid and clear. All the hopes and all the promises of a Church renewed by the Vatican Council were among the graces placed upon us that day. Each in our own way saw a Church moving forward, fresh and revitalized. Even then we were beginning to hear the voices of women and others who had been alienated. But the words we so eagerly wanted to preach surely drowned them out.

We were, after all, trained to be priests, not prophets. So we were not able to see the impending "graying" of the priesthood, the fewer numbers of ordained priests who would follow us, the polarization of the people of God, and the mean-spirited name-calling that would lay pressure upon us well beyond what we would have expected.

Despite our different styles and chosen ministries, we seem to have done a creditable job. We have reconstructed prison ministry, written books, preached at a cardinal's funeral, chaired councils and priest associations, and much more.

Just imagine the number of times we've answered the phone only to be asked the time of the eight o'clock Mass. We have been graced to baptize, to marry, and to bury incredible numbers of people, often laughing and crying at the same ceremony. We've preached so well that we know it could only have been God's grace working through us. And we've embarrassed ourselves at times by an astonishing lack of faith.

We made sure that the very first of our blessings after the ordination ceremony went to our parents, acknowledging their love and the grace they had given to us. Since then we have been privileged to bless countless others, and most of us have sprinkled our parents' coffins with holy water—a final blessing.

The future of our style of priesthood remains uncertain. The Holy Spirit is surely working overtime on our Church at this moment in history. But we have been so graced that we cannot help but trust in that movement of the Spirit in our Church and in our lives, a movement first symbolized by all those hands pressed down on our heads.

Stories of God's Sense of Humor

We make God laugh. We must, because although we are made in God's own image, we are incredibly imperfect. It is a shame we have decided to designate everything godly as serious. Our own laughter can reflect the fun God has in watching us struggle through life. The stuff of growing up makes us laugh

Jesus said to the servants, "Fill the jars with water," and they filled them to the brim. "Draw some out now," he told them, "and take it to the steward." They did this; the steward tasted the water, and it had turned into wine.

~ JOHN 2:7–9

when we look back on it. Good friends make us laugh, even in hard times. In fact, we can find cause for laughter anywhere in God's creation—in friends departing, in lasagna gone bad, and in piano practice. Even the crabby voice of a neighbor can help us join in God's mirth and reflect God's joy.

being brothers

WHEN WE WERE GROWING UP, MY BROTHERS AND
I slept in the same bedroom in two big double beds.
Joe (the oldest) and I were in one bed; Phil and Tony,
the middle two, were in the other. The upstairs rules
were simple. If I accidentally crossed from my side of
the bed onto his side, Joe felt that he had the right
to whale on me, and I couldn't yell out in pain. I
couldn't yell because the main downstairs rule was
that there would be no yelling from upstairs. If we
made too much noise, of any kind, Mom would
come upstairs and spank us. It was kind of a no-win
situation for me as the youngest. But not completely.
On those rare occasions when Mom did spank us, I,
being the youngest, would get a light tap on my
backside, and my oldest brother next to me would
feel the heat of her anger on his. In my mind, there
was some justice in the world after all.

One night our pillow fighting took us out of our beds. When we heard Mom's quick footsteps on the stairs, we panicked and slid ourselves under the nearest set of covers. Unfortunately I ended up on Joe's side of the bed. I should have known his giggling meant that he, under my side of the covers, had just gotten the tap that was meant for me. With the sheets over my head and expecting the usual light touch, I yelled so loudly when I got Joe's smacks that all three of my brothers fell out of bed laughing. It was a setup all along. In her surprise, even Mom laughed.

Somehow we grew up to be good friends, and our closeness was never more evident than in times of crisis when one of us was challenged or in trouble. After all, that is the Italian way. *La familia* always came first.

Once when I was driving home for Sunday pasta, running late after a number of Masses and baptisms, I impatiently cut off another car on Lake Shore Drive. I didn't realize how mad the other driver was until his bumper tapped mine from behind. He continued to do this, a little harder at each successive stoplight. I panicked and started driving faster, taking side streets and then alleys, trying to get away from him. But he stayed on my tail. I grew more frightened by the minute.

I finally pulled into the alley behind my parents' home. To my relief, my brothers' cars were already parked there. I leaned on my car's horn until one of my nieces came out on the porch. I shouted for her to get my brothers. They came running out just as the other car pulled up behind mine. The driver must have seen them and decided against whatever it was he was planning to do. He threw the car into reverse and drove off. When the four of us walked into the house, Mom asked what had happened. One of my brothers simply said, "You don't want to know" and we left it at that. No doubt about it, no matter how old you get, it's great having three older brothers.

These were the same three brothers who came up to the seminary, thirty-five miles from home, to take me out and teach me how to drink wine "in small portions" the night before my ordination. It didn't work. We drank so much wine I honestly didn't expect to see them at the ceremony the next day. But they were there. We always have been there for one another.

A few years later, one of them let me share the sacrament of reconciliation with him in the hospital the night before his surgery. And because I promised that I would tell him everything, it fell to me the next day to give him the news that had our whole family in shock: he had cancer.

I sat beside another brother while the doctor told him that his cancer had probably spread so widely that he would be dead in six months. This brother didn't want the sacrament of reconciliation the night before his surgery. So we just talked, and when we were done I quickly gave him absolution before he knew what I was doing. Don't judge me. I was doing it as much for me as for him. But the next day I was able to tell him after the surgery that the diagnosis had been wrong. He was cancer-free.

Over the years I have been privileged to share many special moments with my brothers. We laughed at my ordination when I made my oldest brother pay me the twenty-five-dollar bet he had made ten years prior that I would never make it through all those years of seminary. There were also the births of my nieces and nephew and then the births of their children. How proud I was of one of my brothers when he risked the loss of his own good name to protect the employees he had hired. He stood up for the right against great odds and won. I couldn't be prouder of them and the accomplishments of their lives.

The four of us recently gathered for my oldest brother's retirement. The reality that two of my brothers have children who are married and that one brother is even a grandfather three times over still astounds me. In my eyes we are still the "four boys," fussing and fighting, yet always watching one another's backs. And that will always give me great comfort.

When I look back at the times we've been together, what I remember most is the warmth of the laughter we've shared. The intimacy of being brothers has allowed us to acknowledge one another's foibles and relax in the comfort of being ourselves.

Wouldn't it be good to have that kind of relationship with God, where we can be comfortable enough to laugh together? I'm certain that our actions make God pause and chuckle with great frequency. It would be nice, at those moments, to simply join in.

laughing through the tears

BEST FRIENDS ARE RARE AND PRECIOUS. AND oh, how we want them to be with us our whole life. When a friend dies, we feel that the loss is permanent and cannot be healed. But I have come to believe that the relationship can continue, even after death, if we are open to it. Perhaps it is a bit of a preview of the resurrection. Whatever it is, it can be joyous to the point of laughter, even when there are tears. I was able to learn this even before my best friend died.

Knowing that he was going to die, Jim planned his wake and funeral. The holy-card memento he selected to be printed was the face of the laughing Jesus. It was the same one we had discovered many years ago in a small religious-goods store in northern California.

I was a teacher back then and always searching for something unique for my classroom bulletin boards. So I bought a large poster of Jesus throwing his head back in a fit of laughter, his teeth and his humanity showing. The poster had hardly been up one school day when the art teacher complained to the principal that it was irreverent, in bad taste, and—even worse—poor art. I was able to defend my sovereignty in my own classroom, and Jesus remained there laughing all year long.

The image now returned these many years later at a time when I was finding it very hard to laugh.

As circumstances—or God's loving intervention—would have it, Jim's brother arrived from England to be with him just a day before he took a turn for the worse. Death was imminent. The whole family decided to spend what would be Jim's last night in his room with him. They needed to be alone with him, and I, somewhat helplessly, got ready to leave. I wanted to be of help in some way. So when the brother from England realized that he had no toothbrush or contact-lens solution, I quickly offered to pick them up for him.

It's not easy to find a drugstore open at midnight on a cold January night. When I finally did, I took out the list of items that had been given to me and started searching from aisle to aisle. But I started to think about Jim at home, probably dying, and I began to cry. My tears caused one of my contact lenses to fall out.

Now, blind in one eye and tears blurring my vision in the other, I was forced to sit on the floor in the middle of an aisle, put all my items down, and grope around for the missing lens. As I sat there crying I suddenly remembered that picture of Jesus laughing and realized that if Jim were there with me, he'd find all of this very funny. I looked up then and saw a woman who had stopped in her tracks when she found me blocking the aisle. I saw the frightened expression on her face—and began to laugh.

So there I was, sitting on the floor of a drugstore late at night, stuff scattered all around me, squinting like a maniac, laughing and crying at the same time. I must have been an unforgettable sight. Until I finally found that contact lens, nobody dared come down that aisle.

Jim did die early the next morning. But because I felt he was with me in the drugstore I was very confident that I'd be feeling his presence at other times. And that has been the case.

Quite often, when I gather with others who were close to Jim, we talk about him, about his illness and untimely death. Then the funny stories begin. All of us seem to have favorites.

Ironically, my stories about Jim involve life and death and tears and sorrow. It is as if I can't get away from those connections. So I'll reminisce about the day Jim was standing in the back of church as the pastor was finishing the funeral of a gentle, retired priest. Jim had grown very fond of the old fellow and was standing there with tears in his eyes. At that moment, a parishioner walked into church and, seeing the funeral in progress and the grief on Jim's face, asked him who had died. Jim told him somberly that it was Fr. Chester. The parishioner then asked, with all sincerity and concern, "Was it something serious?" to which Jim could only reply, "Death usually is." Then Jim started to chuckle, leaving the parishioner perplexed.

A few years after Jim's death, his dear mother died. As I stood in the back of the church at the end of her funeral, I could not help but overhear two little Irish ladies who were walking hand in hand out of the church. They looked at the two statues of Mary, one set up by the Puerto Rican community and one by the Mexican community. One of the ladies turned to the other and said in the thickest of brogues, "Well, will you look at them two. They must be here for all the foreigners." As I started to laugh I could swear I heard Jim chuckle as well.

Sorrow and happiness, tears and laughter, are often parts of the Resurrection journey we are taking. God is there alongside us, crying with us but also showing us joyful laughter. And sometimes both at the same time.

the gift of martyrdom

MOST PORTRAITS OF SAINTS ARE QUITE
solemn. Some saints are portrayed with their eyes
rolling up to heaven in ecstasy. Most have their hands
folded piously in prayer. Once, in a museum, I got all
excited looking at a painting of what I thought was
Saint Francis of Assisi flying a kite in the shape of a
crucifix. I learned to my embarrassment that it was a
portrait of him receiving the stigmata. Paintings of
martyrs are often unusual. They are depicted holding
or carrying something that was a symbol of the martyrdom they endured, such as the sword that beheaded
them. It's interesting that over the centuries some of
these symbols evolved into objects, such as twin
loaves of bread. Unless you know the martyr's story,
you might be led to believe that he or she was kneaded
to death.

The Church has a rich heritage of martyrs that
leads clear up to the present. At this time in history

there are courageous and faith-filled people dying for their beliefs in many places throughout the world. Most of us will not have our faith tested in such a way; our lives are fairly comfortable. But part of me believes that God does test us in smaller ways, sometimes in good-humored ways. Some situations we may never recognize as tests.

A few years back, I visited a couple I had recently married. She was a strikingly beautiful bride. He was one of my former high school students. They made a very cute couple. I felt good, knowing that they were happy and that their lives had come together. So I genuinely looked forward to having dinner at their home. But I had to cancel dinner at the last minute because of an emergency. I don't like to do that, but sometimes it just happens. When I called them, she said not to worry. We immediately set another date.

When that second date arrived, I was able to keep the appointment. I entered their home and guessed that I was the first real guest they had entertained for dinner. Everything was new—the silverware, the china, the crystal, the tablecloth, the napkins. The smell of baking lasagna filled the air. I have found that when you're an Italian priest, most people feel the need to cook you an Italian meal. And everyone believes they can make lasagna. Consequently,

I've eaten some pretty bad lasagna over the years. But I am getting ahead of my story.

We sat for a while having predinner drinks, and I confessed to being very hungry. When we finally did gather for dinner, she brought a beautiful pan of lasagna to the table. As she placed a large, bubbling, cheesy piece onto my plate I once again apologized for the late cancellation of our first dinner engagement. The bride told me that it was no problem at all. She had made this very lasagna the week before we were scheduled to get together. And she had defrosted it and was ready to put it in the oven when I called. So she had simply put it back into the freezer and refrozen it until today.

I'm sure that the smile left my face as red flags started waving before my eyes. All that my mother had taught me about food spoilage came back to me line and verse as I looked at the ricotta cheese, the chunks of sausage, and the bright red sauce. This lovely young girl was innocently serving me poison that looked and smelled delicious. And I had just expressed how hungry I was.

What to do? Do I suddenly put down my plate and proclaim that I've developed a taste for Chinese and that we should order out? Or do I feign a sudden, severe attack of the gout, for which lasagna is not recommended? Do I tell the truth and embarrass a new bride trying so hard to impress both her pastor and her husband? Or do I just trust in God, take a deep breath, and eat the lasagna? I chose the last option. I testified to how great it tasted even as I desperately spread it around my plate and patted it down, trying to make it look as though I had eaten more than I had.

Later that night I found myself going from bedroom to bathroom, groaning. I wanted to call the couple to see if they were all right and if it was really just my imagination, which I seriously doubted. In my fevered state I started to hallucinate. I knew in my heart that I had tried to do the right thing. And figuring I was going to die because of it, a vision of the statue of me, now a martyred saint, flashed before me. For all eternity I would be standing there in bronze, one hand on my stomach in pain, the other holding a large pan of lasagna, the cause of my demise. A most gruesome martyrdom.

Fortunately, by morning I had pretty much recovered. And in retrospect, I would argue that I made the only right and kind choice. God does test us in gentle ways. And sometimes God puts us in laughable situations. Perhaps this is because God needs a break from all the serious concerns that take up so much time. Maybe we become a kind of heavenly comic relief.

have a good day

IN MY NEVER-ENDING SEARCH FOR THE PERFECT
Christmas gift, I have resorted to becoming a catalog
shopper. And while it helps me solve the problem of
dealing with parking, crowds, snow and slush, and
interminably long lines, it also leaves me with a virtual avalanche of mail starting around the first of
August. Fresh fruit from Australia, lean buffalo ribs
from Texas, rustic ornaments from Vermont, auto
accessories from Germany, and unimaginable numbers
of other exotic items entice me with beautiful pictures
and descriptions. Choices are so hard to make.

One year I thought that I had come up with
the perfect gift. It came from one of the most desir-
able (read "expensive") catalogs I had received. It was
such a good idea, in fact, that I ordered one for each
of my three older brothers. After all, who could resist
a scale that actually said hello, magically vocalized

your weight, told you how much you had gained or lost since you last stepped on it, and then finished the encounter with a cheerful "Have a good day"? This scale could store in its memory an entire family's previous weights. It seemed almost too good to be true—a scale to bond with.

Imagine my surprise not only when my brothers were decidedly unenthusiastic about their gifts but also when they communicated to me in various ways that it was the stupidest gift in the annals of my checkered gift-giving career. As time went by I received reports about this awful gift. It seems that visiting guests would sneak up onto it only to be scared off, embarrassed by the unexpected voice. One brother even insisted that when someone's weight went up, the voice took on a decidedly mocking tone.

The following Christmas I opened the present from my brothers—to find a talking scale just like the one I had given them. Their comment: "Well, you liked that one you gave us so much, we all thought you'd like one yourself."

And, you know, at first I did. But after a while that voice did begin to take on a life of its own, always there when I called it out of its own little world inside the scale. Sometimes months would pass before I stepped onto it. And it seemed that every time I did, it would respond, "You have gained three pounds."

Occasionally it was more. Seldom was it the same. Never was it less.

Finally, on doctor's orders, I purchased a treadmill and started to exercise. I needed to reverse that dangerous trend. But it was the holidays. I figured that, with all I would be eating, just holding my own would be enough. Dieting would start in earnest after the New Year's celebrations. So I was pleasantly surprised when the scale greeted me with a lower weight than I expected, even with all the heavy holiday eating. I didn't go up a pound no matter what I ate.

I decided that this was an excellent time to make a doctor's appointment. I pictured how proud he would be to see my weight lowered and holding despite all my eating. Clearly exercise was the key. It was so easy. And it was amazing what ten minutes of walking on the treadmill every other day could do.

I was confident as the exam began. Having taken off every stitch of clothing except for what would keep me decent in front of the nurse, I proudly stepped onto the doctor's scale. I waited. The nurse said, "Push the bar." I did. She said, "No, to the right." I did. "More," she said. I did. "Move another bar," she said. "You must be wrong," I said. She said, "Move it." I did. Finally satisfied, she recorded my weight. How could it be a full twenty pounds higher than my last visit and thirty pounds more than my talking scale had proudly boasted earlier in the day? "Your scale must be broken," I pleaded. "Doctor's scales are never broken" was her heartless response.

So after a deserved tongue-lashing from my doctor I went home. I looked at the traitor scale. My cat walked by. I picked it up, all eighteen pounds, and placed it on the scale. "Hello," the scale sang out cheerfully and then proceeded to give the same weight it had been giving me for the last two months. The scale wasn't omniscient. It was just plain broken. I picked up the scale and threw it in the garbage. And as I stalked back toward the house I could hear it say one last time, "Have a good day." Was it laughing at me, telling me to lighten up?

I had been counting on that voice to be accurate even when deep down I knew I was only fooling myself. So I let it be true until I was confronted with reality.

It's like trying to figure out if it's God's voice we are hearing or if we are hearing only what we want to hear. We are so foolish that we can't hear God's chuckling.

Chances are, if we are hearing exactly what we want to hear, it's probably not God's voice. We take ourselves way too seriously. Certainly God challenges us. But God also playfully laughs at our foibles and inconsistencies. God wants us to laugh along, because the best laughter is always shared. So listen for God, and let go and have a good day.

sleeping in the park

MONDAY MORNINGS ARE JUST NOT GOOD TIMES for me to deal with people on the telephone. I seem psychologically incapable of communicating with people if I can't look them in the eye. My secretary knows this quirk and does her very best to screen my calls. She knows that by 10 A.M. I am back in the groove and can handle just about anything. So when she warned me early one Monday morning that the woman on the line was a neighbor who sounded quite upset, my instincts urged me to have her take a message so I could handle it later. But I didn't. I took the call, which was my first mistake.

"You don't know me," the voice on the phone said, and red flag number one flashed before my eyes. "I've been your neighbor for months." Red flag number two. "I really like all you do for the community, but . . ." Red flag number three. "You know, I don't go to church, but I'm a religious person." Red flag number four.

"Just what is it you are trying to tell me?" I asked. Any more red flags and I'd feel as though it were May Day in the Kremlin. "It's those disgusting street people in your park. You know they aren't homeless at all. They are just a bunch of drunken bums. I know." I wondered how she knew. Who knows? Maybe she drank with them at the local establishment on the corner. "They sleep in your park and scare us honest people away." Since when did sleeping become dishonest? "You should have a rule that says no sleeping in the park."

At that point, I broke in and explained how hard it would be to enforce a no-sleeping rule. I wasn't about to go out there on a regular basis to make sure everyone on the benches was upright and conscious. Besides, the park was always filled with nannies and their carriages, college students from the university down the street, elderly folk from one of the local senior buildings taking a walk and sitting awhile, couples obviously in love, and kids just being kids.

I didn't want to talk to her anymore. So I recklessly invited her to call the police whenever she saw something in the park that she thought was dangerous or illegal. I told her to feel free to say that she was calling in the pastor's name. That would turn out to be my second mistake.

A few weeks later, I had a break of an hour or so before any of my evening appointments. It was one of those incredibly mild, early summer evenings. Since I had been cooped up in my office all day, I decided to sit in the park and work on the next Sunday's homily. The park was empty and quiet except for the gentle trickling of the fountain. The breeze was warm. My stomach was full. I started to nod off. I remained upright, even if I might have been listing a bit to my left.

Abruptly I was jolted awake by two uniformed Chicago police officers. The hand on my shoulder made me jump to my feet. In a panic, I asked what the problem was. They told me gruffly that I had to clear out of the park. I asked them why, since I was the pastor who had raised the money and built the park just a few years earlier. They told me that was impossible, since the call had come from someone complaining in the pastor's name about the people drinking and sleeping in the park and scaring everyone else away. I pleaded guilty to having fallen asleep. I had no container of drink with me. And while I couldn't deny that the sight of me asleep on the park bench might scare away some particularly squeamish people, I did point out that the park had been empty when I sat down.

It took me a little while, but I was finally able to clarify who I was, and the police left. I realized that I had failed to get the name or number of the voice on the phone, the nosy neighbor who had caused this trouble. If I could have, I would have called her back and said, at least, "Get a life!"

But eventually I was struck by the irony of what had just taken place. It was really quite funny. After all, if she truly was afraid of me sleeping on the bench *I* had installed in the park *I* had built on the property of which *I* was pastor, of course she would be frightened of disturbed street people.

She has never called back or stopped to identify herself to me when I was sitting in the park, awake.

No wonder God laughs with and at us. We are made in God's image, and so is the world we live in. Yet we find ourselves at such odds with this world and with each other—and over the silliest things sometimes. I think that God designs certain humorous situations just to wake us up to see God's face in someone else, in some setting we don't expect.

Stories of God's Forgiveness

Somehow we have allowed guilt to become an important tenet of life and faith. We have made guilt more prominent in our thinking than God's forgiveness. Yet, without that forgiveness, guilt will only lead us to despair. Knowing we are forgiven helps us learn from long-ago mistakes and brings others back to God. It

> Jesus said to the paralytic,
> "Courage, my child, your sins are
> forgiven." And at this some scribes
> said to themselves, "This man is
> blaspheming." Knowing what was
> in their minds Jesus said, "Why do
> you have such wicked thoughts in
> your hearts?" Now, which of these is
> easier: to say, 'Your sins are forgiv-
> en,' or to say, 'Get up and walk?'"
>
> ~ **MATTHEW 9:2–5**

can help us forgive people who have hurt us. It can ease the pain and bring healing to those who are hurting. It should not surprise us that we are forgiven by God. But we are often slow to recognize the reflections of this forgiveness.

a pizza delivered

I'M LIVING PROOF THAT THE SAYING "CHALK IT up to experience" can be quite a dangerous way to go through life. Just imagine someone saying that as he runs a red light the first day he has a driver's license. Or think of a surgeon saying that as he nicks an important artery. What would we think if we heard such a statement from an air traffic controller who was watching two blips heading directly toward each other on the screen in front of her?

How can we ever experience God's loving forgiveness if we won't even admit we were wrong? How can we grow if we refuse to admit that what we've done or failed to do was hurtful to ourselves or to others? And how can we become better persons if in the name of psychological health we try to bury the harm we've done, packing it away and leaving only the "happy" and "good" thoughts to dance in our psyches? A simple but profound experience early in my ministry has stayed with me and illustrates well our need for forgiveness.

With much promise and hope, Johnny left the orphanage for a foster home. His birth mother had abandoned him, and after he spent years in various institutions, a childless couple had agreed to take him into their home as a foster son. The initial adjustment had its problems. The couple did not have enough experience to cope with the problems that emerged. They wanted a quick fix when what they needed was long-term help and support. What they got was me, a seminarian who was volunteering at the orphanage. I was sent to meet with Johnny and his foster parents weekly. I came with a lot of enthusiasm and no experience. And that proved to be a lethal combination.

At the beginning, things seemed to get better. Johnny was happier and the couple more relaxed. They continued to complain about small things, but by and large I was pretty proud of my handiwork. But I arrived at their home one cold winter night to find that another foster child had been brought into the family. He looked as though he could be Johnny's twin brother, only three years younger. And, compared to Johnny's behavior, this child seemed to function perfectly. A whole new level of tension developed, and the situation grew far more complex than I could possibly handle. No matter what I nervously attempted to do, each succeeding week it became clearer to me that Johnny was being set aside and the new child was stepping in as his replacement.

I should have gone immediately to someone with more experience. I should have challenged the foster parents and questioned how they were managing the situation. I should have realized that I was in way over my head. But I didn't. As the situation grew worse I found more and more excuses to miss our weekly appointments. I had to study for exams. Or it looked like snow. Or I had a cold. After a while I just stopped calling or going at all. It is still painful for me to admit this totally irresponsible behavior. Did I feel guilty? Yes, initially. But with everything else I was doing, it wasn't that hard to forget about Johnny and his family.

At this time I was also a student chaplain at the juvenile detention center in Chicago. One day I went to my assigned unit, and there sat Johnny in his prison uniform. My heart lurched with embarrassment, shame, and no little fear. I did not want him to see me. I knew that I couldn't face his anger. But I was stuck. The guard wouldn't be back to open the door for forty-five minutes.

When Johnny looked up and saw me, he waved. I was surprised to see that he was smiling. I wanted very much to start with an apology. But before I could speak, he looked at me innocently and said,

"I guess I owe you a pizza." I realized that the last time I saw him, months ago at his house, we had agreed that if he didn't get into trouble that week, I'd buy him a pizza when I came the next week. But if he did get into trouble, he'd buy me one. Johnny's simple statement hurt more than if he had yelled at me or snubbed me or even punched me. His matter-of-fact response left me speechless. All I could do was listen as he told how things had gotten so bad at home that he'd had to run away. He said that the day after our visit he was scheduled to go to a youth camp in Montana. I lamely tried to apologize for having abandoned him. His response once again was, "I guess I owe you a pizza." And then my time in the unit was up and I had to leave. I never saw Johnny again.

Back at the seminary that night, I couldn't get to sleep. I finally wandered into the chapel. I was sorry for botching up Johnny's life so badly. Part of me felt that I should be punished. And part of me needed to be forgiven. All of me didn't want to ever let anything like that happen again. So I asked for God's forgiveness. But I realized that just telling God I was sorry would not be enough, for me at least. I promised myself that wherever my ministry took me, I would never abandon the Johnnys I was called upon to serve and help.

Every once in a while I wonder what happened to Johnny. My ministry is busy, rich, and full.

It would be quite dramatic if the doorbell rang one day and there was an unordered pizza being delivered—from someone named Johnny. But that has never happened.

God's forgiveness has come to me through countless other opportunities to help people, to be there when they needed me to not give up on them. Occasionally I have messed up. But quite often I have managed to do the right thing. And this is, after all, how God's forgiveness works. God gives us opportunities to learn from our mistakes, to grow and not repeat them. Thank God for such forgiveness.

a first reconciliation

BEING A PASTOR, IT IS HARD FOR ME TO STAY
current on all the new liturgical, sacramental, and
theological trends that develop and ultimately filter
their way into the pastoral practice of the parish. I
have grown to be more pragmatic than dogmatic. If
something is working well and reaching the people
of God, why change it? If it no longer works, what
do we need to do to make it effective?

I enjoy how our parish has been celebrating
the first sacrament of reconciliation. I am convinced
that the children who share with me their desire for
God's forgiveness are no more capable of serious sinfulness than I am of running a four-minute mile. Yet
their sincerity and innocent trust in a loving God
always move me. Their example increases my own
desire for God's forgiveness in my life.

The sacrament is set in the context of an
evening prayer service. The children sit with their

parents in the security of a caring embrace. After a song and a reading, the children come forward and sit with me and help me with my homily, explaining to everyone present why this is truly a joyful celebration. Because God loves us and forgives our faults and sins, we have all the more reason to live good and holy lives. Children are able to express these concepts in a simple, beautiful way. They move quickly past guilt.

The parents are then invited to bring their children individually to one of the priests. Parents present their child and reassure them that they will be praying for us during this, the child's first experience of the sacrament of reconciliation.

When every child has finished sharing the sacrament and the families are all gathered together again, we turn the tables a bit. We tell everyone that the priests are going back to the reconciliation rooms. Now we invite the children to bring to the sacrament those parents who have been touched by God's grace as they have watched and felt the faith of their children.

What a special moment—a child leading parents to the priest, introducing them with sincerity, and assuring the parents that they will now be praying for them. Some adults have been away from this sacrament for many years. They may not be sure of what to say or how to say it. But they do, and often this results in moments of tremendous healing and forgiveness.

One mother broke down in tears. The child she had adopted brought her in to me. This child was beautiful, but always serious. He seldom smiled. As the mother cried she shared her story. Let me share it without breaking the seal of the sacrament. I'll change the details but not the truth.

Unmarried, on the fast track, and working for the district attorney's office in a large West Coast city, she found herself on a team prosecuting the parent of a four-year-old child. This parent's abuse had been horrible. The evidence was overwhelming and the conviction easy. In the course of the trial, she felt a genuine bond grow between her and the child.

Adoption happened. But it was not easy, even with a fresh start in a new city. Love does heal, but it takes a lot of time. Even with his first Eucharist just weeks away, the child questioned God's love for him. He would not let anyone touch him. The mother would feel his pain and see his scars and be filled with hatred and anger toward those who had stolen a child's innocence. She was frightened by those feelings. She was also frightened about the future of this child she had grown to love so dearly.

We talked, she mostly. I merely assured her of God's loving forgiveness for all her hard feelings. I told her that God was certainly blessing her heroic efforts. I said that the more she let God into her own heart, the more the child's heart would soften. We ended with the words of absolution.

As all the families gathered for the final prayer and song, I noticed that nearly every child was sitting with a parent's arm around him or her in a natural gesture of protection and affection. We were singing, "Come back to me with all your heart. Don't let fear keep us apart." As the song continued, this young child—who had been so abused he never wanted anyone, even his new mother, to touch him—slowly leaned over and rested his head on her shoulder. "Long have I waited for your coming home to me." This was a lesson in the power of God's reconciling and forgiving love. If God can be so forgiving, so must we. And when that happens, what miracles can and do take place!

I encouraged each of the families not to go directly home. I wanted them to continue the celebration of God's forgiveness over a hot fudge sundae or a banana split. I wanted them to smile and laugh and feel as good as I felt just then. My prayer was that they would never forget this night of first reconciliation and how powerful God's forgiveness really is.

We always hope that the first sacrament of reconciliation will become the first step of a life journey. What a wonderful journey that can be when we walk in the confidence of a loving God at our side who forgives, heals, and encourages us.

the hounds of heaven

THOSE OF US WHO PREACH ARE OFTEN ACCUSED
of concentrating too much on hell and damnation
rather than on heaven and forgiveness. But there is a
very good reason for this. When all is said and done,
it is much easier to speak about hell than about
heaven. After all, the picture of hell as fire and brim-
stone, or even as isolation, is deeply ingrained in the
psyches of most believers. Classic literature and art
are filled with images of hell.

Heaven, on the other hand, is harder to grasp.
If we try to visualize merely approaching a God who
knows everything we've done or thought—well, it is
beyond our entire frame of reference. None of the
words to describe entering God's loving presence are
in our dictionaries or memories or dreams. Our very
humanness makes hell a visible reality and heaven a
shrouded mystery.

The parish's annual blessing of pets was the usual cacophony of barks, hisses, meows, squawks, and other noises emanating from hundreds of animals held dear by their adoptive owners (or families, as some prefer to be called). I am continually amazed at the love we are able to share with God's creatures and the affection we are given in return. Dogs of every size, shape, and voice, cats and kittens peering out of cages or wrapped in loving arms, birds and fish, turtles dry and wet, rabbits and mice, a nervous ferret, and even a praying mantis (how appropriate!) filled the park behind the church. Noah would have been proud. We said prayers, invoked blessings, sang songs, and ate animal crackers. The crowd was slow to leave as people stood talking and the animals sniffed one another curiously.

A young man no older than twenty-five came up to me, holding a dog so old that its every breath seemed a challenge. Its eyes were clouded with blindness. Its coat was sparse and spotty. When the young man set it down, it was barely able to stand. More than one veterinarian had suggested to the young man that his dog be put out of its misery. But he was unable to do it. The dog had been with him since he was a child of seven. They had grown up together. But now, no matter what the young man decided, the end was coming, and it would not be easy for him to face.

"Are there dogs in heaven?" he asked, with as much earnestness as any question directed to me in recent memory. I just looked at him as his eyes filled with tears. I gently patted the head of his old, faithful companion. This was no time for a theological presentation.

So I stood and listened as he told me the history of a boy and his dog and their lifelong relationship. He tried hard to show that the dog had never been mean or malicious, even if it had chewed up a shoe or two over the years. It was as though he wanted the dog to be forgiven any of its failings. And the dog, seeming to appreciate all that his friend was saying, attempted a feeble lick of the young man's face.

"Heaven," I said, "is where we are with God and all our loved ones for all eternity, and where our sins and our failings are forgiven." I could see that these words were not enough for him. I had to say more. "You and your dog," I continued. "How could this loving relationship end with death? God's forgiveness extends to all his creatures. Why shouldn't your dog be waiting for you, tail wagging, when the time comes?"

So, for better or for worse, in one fast swoop the gate of heaven swung open to all the pets that have ever given people joy and happiness, companionship and love. What else could I do at that moment?

Anything else would have been cruel and made God out to be uncaring and unforgiving. And who really knows for sure? I am betting heavily that good old Saint Peter, the keeper of the keys, had on his fishing boat a loyal pooch that traveled with him to Rome. In any case, Saint Francis of Assisi is there to put in a good word for the animals barking, squeaking, and squawking at the gate.

Whatever the theological reality, it seemed that my few words brought a great deal of comfort to the young man. That was all I had intended to do. The love and forgiveness of God now filled what had been a void of uncertainty. "Did you hear that, boy?" he asked. "I always knew that God would let you be there waiting for me." I'd like to say that the dog appeared to understand and wagged his tail or barked in response. But it was too weak, fortunately for me. I did not need a co-conspirator.

After a while, all the animals cleared out of the park, most of them leading the owners who had brought them. It was clear that the simple blessing shared by these pets and their owners had meant a great deal. Everyone went home happy, the young man especially, and me as well.

There are many reasons, some heroic and most good, to want to go to heaven. I can't wait to see just how we will all be united, especially with those we have loved in our earthly life—divine, canine, human, and otherwise—and how we will all be brought together by a God who has forgiven us all our faults and failings.

a message from an angel

I AM ALL FOR FREEDOM OF SPEECH AND
freedom of the press and all those other wonderful
freedoms guaranteed by the Bill of Rights. But I've
found that sometimes being a public person sets you
up to be attacked by those who would abuse those
freedoms. And when that happens, the last thing on
my mind is a desire to protect our precious rights. At
those times, forgiving and turning the other cheek
are not high on my list of responses. Those are the
times when "Forgive us our trespasses as we forgive
those who trespass against us" becomes for me an
insurmountable challenge.

A few years back, after I had been quoted in a
magazine article, a group that did not agree with
what I'd said went on the offensive. All of a sudden
this group leafleted the audience at every place I was
scheduled to speak, no matter what the topic. Even
though this treatment made for a more sympathetic

and receptive audience, I was disturbed by the hateful and insulting content of the leaflet. And I never knew who my accusers were, since they always hid behind the cover of anonymity.

One early summer Sunday morning, I stepped out of church into the sunshine after celebrating the Eucharist, only to notice a bright goldenrod sheet of paper on the windshield of every car in my line of vision. As I stood there wondering what new restaurant was opening in the neighborhood, someone wordlessly handed me one of the sheets. It was the same leaflet that had been following me around. But this time it was where I lived and worked—my home. This upset me. When I returned to the rectory later that night, I found the parish answering machine filled with messages of support. There were also many notes in the front mail slot, all from parishioners and neighbors, to encourage me. They wanted me to know of their support and their anger about the leaflets on their cars. All this made me feel better, but I was still quite angry at the perpetrators.

A few months later, on another beautiful Sunday morning, I came upon someone placing those same leaflets on the cars. This time it was being done right on parish property, in our parking lot. She was quite an attractive woman in her twenties. Her look sure didn't fit the words in the leaflet. But I invited her to leave the private property on which she was trespassing—or

I'd call the police and have her arrested. She ignored me. She wouldn't tell me who she was or who she represented, so I got right in her face and started calling her a coward, among other things. I wanted to intimidate her, to scare her off.

But I stopped dead in my tracks when I noticed that she was wearing one of those little "angel on my shoulder" pins. Earlier in the week I had been shopping for my mother's birthday gift. She had wanted such an angel, and I had bought her the exact same one that this young lady was wearing.

I stopped my speech so abruptly, the young woman must have thought I had tripped some internal circuit. What happened was that she was no longer a symbol of all that was wrong with the Church—all the divisiveness, the holier-than-thou pharisaism infecting it. No longer was she someone breaking the law or even someone who dared to dislike me and what I said. That little angel on her shoulder turned her into a person as real as my own mother.

I stepped back and softly invited her into the rectory to talk. She looked surprised, but she declined. I asked her why she felt compelled to do what she was doing. After all, she didn't really know me or understand where I stood on so many issues. I wanted her to get to know me better before she passed judgment. But she declined to answer. All she would say was that she felt she had to do what she was doing.

And so I assured her that, once off our property, she was certainly free to do whatever she desired. By then, the anger on both sides had been defused.

When parishioners started coming up to me, once again really upset about the leaflets, they seemed surprised at my calm demeanor. They expected to find me angry and upset. But I was focusing on the young woman who believed so strongly in what she was doing. I knew that we would never come to any agreement on what we believed or how we acted on those beliefs.

I realized then that the only response left to me was to be loving and forgiving. The insidious thing about this last round of leafleting was that it had nearly brought me down to a level of anger and violence that would have ultimately negated all I believe about God's love and God's Spirit protecting the Church.

If it hadn't been for that little angel perched on the young woman's shoulder, my response would have indeed been different. I am sure there are times we hurt God with our sinfulness. But God's forgiveness is always instantaneous and complete. And reconciliation occurs with no strings attached. That is to be expected because God is God and doesn't ever need angel pins to remind him of how to respond. On the other hand, we are human, and sometimes those angels sure do come in handy.

thumping watermelons

WORK WAS ALMOST SACRED TO MY DAD. FOR HIM it was a sign of both responsibility and manhood. It was also the primary way to show others you loved them. It is no wonder, then, that my brothers and I were working in the family grocery store even before our voices began to change.

As we grew older there was a progression in our responsibilities. At first, all we were expected to do was "front the aisles," which meant straightening up the shelves and moving the cans, packages, and bottles forward to be more clearly seen and accessible to the customers. We were also responsible for retrieving wayward shopping carts and taking the empty deposit bottles to the back room. From this we graduated to packing the shoppers' grocery bags—eggs and bread on top, or else. Then we became full-fledged stock boys with our own ink price stampers. At fifteen we were subbing for the men who took care of the fruits and vegetables in the produce department. A year later we were sent to the National Cash Register School for three days, the only males in an all-female class. Truly that was the pinnacle.

I enjoyed working in the produce department the most. Being the youngest, I was bossed around by everyone else. But back in produce I was away from the critical eyes of my family. Better yet, I was near the grapes and cherries, which were just waiting for me to pick at them. I quickly learned to keep the cherry pits in my pocket so that my dad and my uncle wouldn't be able to catch me eating up the profits.

I became very accurate with the scale, and my math skills helped me with the quick calculations necessary when a customer only wanted four oranges and they were selling six for fifty cents. I was trained to always round up and give the store the extra penny. (The answer is forty cents.)

One summer day, however, problems arose when one of the produce workers was on vacation, another on his day off, and the other on his lunch hour. That meant I was left alone with all the fruits and vegetables and customers.

My fears were realized when one of those customers asked me to select a ripe watermelon for her. I very judiciously looked them over, selected a few, and thumped them. I nodded knowledgeably, smiled, and then announced triumphantly which one was the best. The problem was that I had no idea what I was doing. I couldn't distinguish a good thumping sound from a bad one if my life depended on it.

The customer then announced that she wanted only half of the watermelon. Right there— before her eyes and mine—we would see whether or not I had selected the ideal watermelon. She warned me in no uncertain terms that I had better have selected one that was ripe, with little rind, juicy, but with not too many seeds. Just how, I wondered, was my thumping supposed to do all that?

I had no choice. I sliced open the melon. Immediately she informed me that it just wouldn't do. It had too many seeds. So I threw it out and halved another. But after she tasted it, she announced that it wasn't ripe enough. She made a face at the next one, saying that it was much too ripe. The next one had too thick a rind; she hurt her teeth biting into it. By this time, with all her tasting she had eaten probably half a watermelon. So I shouldn't have been surprised when she left without selecting any of the dozen or so that I had cut open.

I looked around and panicked. There were pieces of watermelon and rind, seeds and juice every-where. The garbage bin was filled with discarded melons. What would happen if my dad or my uncle saw the mess I had made? As I was frantically trying to clean everything up I saw my dad. He was heading right toward the produce department and me.

The first thing he said was, "What the hell?" I quickly interrupted him and tried to convince him that this mess wasn't my fault, that everything just got out of control—that he, after all, had taught me that the customer is always right. He just stood there without a word, his look making me feel even more stupid than I must have sounded.

I have never been able to read my father well. Just when I thought I was going to get a major chewing out in front of coworkers and customers, he said, "I know her. You never could have pleased her." And he started helping me clean up the mess. I couldn't believe it. When we were done, he didn't say another word about it and neither did I.

Sometimes forgiveness can happen when we don't even say we are sorry. We make excuses and try to cover our tracks, thinking that we might convince God to accept our version of what happened. Instead God accepts us and shows us we are forgiven by helping us get through the mess we've made—no matter whose fault it was. Often we are surprised by God's forgiving response when we really shouldn't be. We expect God to be less than God. And when God responds, we are left speechless.

Stories of God's Mystery

All too often we choose not to reflect on God in our lives, probably because we sense how tremendously awesome God is, and it frightens us. It shouldn't. In the best of relationships there remains some mystery. Then why not with God? Joy and sorrow side by side, sadness as time passes—these are mysteries. We

No one has ever seen God; it is
the only Son, who is nearest to
the Father's heart, who has made
him known.

~ **JOHN 1:18**

---

experience mystery even as close as our own beating

hearts. But perhaps the greatest mystery of all is the

life to which God calls us. On this we need to reflect

every day of our lives. That isn't always easy.

the christmas tree and the easter cross

IT IS UNFORTUNATE THAT I SOMETIMES
separate the wonderful living reality of the liturgical
year into stagnant components with formal names.
They become Christmas and Easter, "holidays" to be
celebrated. When this happens, writing homilies
becomes difficult, and the results are shallow at best.
I can usually survive on clever word games made
passable by a quarter century's experience.

So it was one recent Christmas. Panic was setting in at 10:30 P.M. on Christmas Eve. My homily for
the midnight and morning Masses was not yet in
shape. So I had to settle for a funny family anecdote
and a catchy phrase: "A celebration of small miracles." Using that, along with the glue of bravado, I
created a pleasing-enough homily for the two Mass
congregations that would fill the church. I did not
know I was preparing myself to encounter the mystery of God's way and how it is so awesomely re-

flected in the connectedness of the seasons of faith. Christmas leads to Easter; the birth of the Savior ultimately leads to Jesus' death and, more important, Jesus' resurrection.

After the service, a woman—whom I'd never seen before and haven't seen since—approached, saying that she had a message for me. She waited patiently while I completed my litany of "Merry Christmases" to members of the congregation as they departed into the cold winter morning. When I finally turned to her and asked what the message might be, she simply said, "You have a lot of work to do, so take care of yourself. You have to get it all done." Then she turned and walked out of church, a belated Gabriel, leaving behind a disturbing and mysterious message.

Just one week later I was stumbling through a passionless New Year's Eve homily, trying vainly to communicate how, in the coming year, we needed to take the risk of pouring out all the blessings God had so lovingly given us during the past year. As I preached I was more than a little distracted by an obviously disturbed young woman (twenty-four? twenty-five? it was hard to tell her age) who throughout the Mass talked to a ragged doll she held in her arms. Some of the parishioners also were uncomfortable with her actions. *Just my luck,* I thought. After a while, a priest can develop a sixth sense about someone with a problem in church. *No mystery here.* This was just what I needed on the last night of the year. I hoped she would just go away.

After Mass I was extinguishing the Christmas candles and unplugging the Italian lights on the trees when she walked around the rapidly emptying church. Finally, she walked right up to me and asked in a gruff voice for a bathroom. Against my better judgement I pointed it out to her. And then I waited. She took her time there and still was not ready to depart.

Standing there, I gauged how stern I would have to be to get her out of the church so I could lock up. I watched her as she walked slowly to the large crucifix at the back of the church and then over to the parish Christmas tree decorated with ornaments brought in by parishioners.

Suddenly, the connection between the tree of Christmas and the cross of Easter hit me somewhere between my hardened heart and my blinded eyes. Even as one mystery revealed itself, another would take its place. Why would God become one like us? Be born into our world? Why would God choose to die on a cross? What does the Resurrection mean?

I realized that, yes, the previous week's mysterious message to me was valid. I did indeed have work to do. But it would be no grand project. No, it would be just some small miracles. That would be my work this year. And the challenge to begin stood before me right then and there. It was all coming together in a special way at that moment. The mystery of the Resurrection began at the moment of Jesus' birth.

The woman touched the tree. I asked her if she wanted an ornament for herself. At first she looked shocked. Then she smiled and asked shyly if indeed she could have one. After I nodded, she asked me which one. A simple wooden carving caught my eye. It was Gabriel blowing his horn, bringing his message. I handed it to her and said that it was a special one. Mystery solved, I started to feel proud of myself.

But then she thanked me, and as we walked out of the church she suddenly showed me her doll and asked me softly if I liked her baby. She gave it a kiss. Oh, my loving God! The tree and the cross together really. What was her pain? I wondered. What was her loss? What had happened in her life that all she had was a doll to hold on to? What, God, could all this mean? Why? How can we sing "Joy to the World" and face the cross of Jesus at the same time? "It's a beautiful baby," I assured her. It was the smallest of miracles. That's all we could share.

holy week mysteries

A FEW YEARS AGO, PALM SUNDAY CAME IN AS warm as everyone hoped Easter would be the following week. After all the Masses and the processions and the choir's annual breakfast and bake sale, I needed the rest of Sunday off. So I joined a few friends, and we headed down to North Michigan Avenue—Chicago's Magnificent Mile, an area resplendent with great restaurants, shops, and movie theaters—to enjoy an early spring evening. It seemed, however, that just about everybody else had the same idea.

In fact, even after dark it was still as crowded as any weekday rush hour. Stores were still open. Movie theaters had long lines, and restaurants were projecting waits of over an hour. We decided to just walk and enjoy the warmth of the air and the sights and sounds of the city.

We passed a New York City–based toy store, one that caters to clientele for whom money is no object. Its shelves were stocked with dolls and games and stuffed animals of all sorts, and its windows were filled with animated figures and various costumed characters greeting people on the street. It seemed that the very contents of the store were overflowing onto the sidewalk.

People were stopping to look at the characters who had come to life. Standing in front of us and extending greetings to everyone passing by were an Easter Bunny of awesome height, a pigtailed Dorothy from *The Wizard of Oz* holding a limp, stuffed Toto, and a cowboy who could put John Wayne to shame.

The children were absolutely mesmerized. They talked to Dorothy in quiet and polite voices, asking the whereabouts of the Tin Man, the Lion, and the Scarecrow. They seemed a little afraid of the cowboy. Maybe it was his six-shooter that made them so timid! But it was the poor Easter Bunny who took the brunt of the curiosity. They poked him (or was it her? it's hard to tell with Easter Bunnies) in the stomach, stomped on his paws, and yanked his tail.

The children themselves were impeccably dressed in designer clothes (which they would quickly outgrow) that certainly cost more than I could imagine. Hair brushed and combed. Expensive brands of athletic shoes. They looked like little adults, so dressed up, but acted like the children they were.

I looked away from them and noticed another child standing outside the bright lights of the toy store's perimeters. This child, with dark skin and unkempt hair, looked very different from the others. His clothes were too short for his tall frame, yet too big for his skinny body. He was leaning against a lamppost as though he were trying to hide behind it. He held a dirty, roughly crafted cardboard box with a hand-painted sign that read, "Shine—50 Cents."

What struck me most about the child were his eyes. They were a mystery. There was absolutely no sparkle in them, no glimpse of hope, and no excitement at seeing the characters come to life. At the age of ten or so, this child looked decades old and very tired.

I was pretty sure he knew intellectually that there was nothing in that toy store he could afford, even after a full day of shining shoes. But I could not begin to understand how knowing that and seeing the other children's happiness would make him feel. Was he sad? Would anger eventually consume him? How could a child so young not be confused by a world so different, yet so nearly his own? Did he wish that he were one of the children playing so excitedly with Dorothy, the cowboy, and the Easter

Bunny? Or was he more cynical, thinking that he was too grown up for all of this?

I looked back at the children in their pre-Easter finery. Parents were getting impatient and beginning to pull them away. The children didn't mind. They had had their fun and now walked away hand in hand with their parents.

By then, the other child had gone, too, walking alone, slightly slumped, into the shadow of the side street. And I wondered if he knew what we would celebrate this week—that Jesus had died for this child because Jesus loved him. Would it remain a mystery to him? Would the Easter message ever mean anything to him—or to anyone else robbed of childhood celebrations?

I went home feeling less Palm Sunday hope and much less Easter Sunday joy. The mystery of Good Friday suddenly enveloped me. Sometimes we forget that, while we can embrace Easter, another person is still in the darkness of the Crucifixion. The mystery is that all of our holy days are meaningful at any one time, and they perfectly fit so many human lives. Perhaps we need to dwell in the day our neighbor dwells in, at least long enough to bring him or her to the next step.

old
snapshots

OUR SOCIETY IS QUICK TO DISPOSE OF
anything old. Companies come out with new prod-
ucts. Corporations publish annual reports that promise new beginnings. We speak of "planned obsoles-
cence" and "downsizing." For most people new is
better, and old is quickly discarded or forgotten. This
is especially true among younger people.

So maybe it's because I am getting older that I
find myself drawn to antique stores. I marvel at what
all that faded stuff still has to say to us today. And,
besides, antique-store owners are usually a tremendously interesting lot.

Recently I came upon a box of dirty old photographs in a small shop that was run by a friendly
gentleman who could easily have qualified as an
antique himself. From the bent wire-rimmed glasses
perched on the tip of his nose to his faded gold pocket watch, he was the picture of everyone's "gramps"

from the twenties or thirties. He quietly watched me spend a good deal of time going through the pictures. Some were formal studio shots still in their original cardboard folders; others were snapshots of various sizes. A small printed sign priced the smaller pictures at a quarter and the larger ones at two dollars.

My attention was diverted suddenly when the owner said in a soft voice, "Bring the box over here, lad." Nobody had called me "lad" in quite a few years, so I responded like an obedient grandchild.

"You're wondering where all these pictures came from, aren't you?" he asked, reading my mind. The question had been on the tip of my tongue.

He explained that most of the items in his shop were bought wholesale from dealers. These dealers would clean out the houses and apartments of people who died with no living relatives or whose families wanted to get rid of everything quickly for one lump price. The dealers would sort through it all and keep the valuable antiques. Small shops like this one could buy what was left over for "dirt cheap," as he said.

Old photographs, unless they were in ornate frames, were usually discarded as worthless. But he'd found that every once in a while someone like me would come in and be enthralled by the mystery of the faded images.

I lifted out a picture of a dapper soldier, his army cap tilted rakishly to one side, his arm around his buddies. "World War II," the old fellow said, "was the biggest thing that ever happened to a lot of guys. They found themselves in faraway places, met exotic women, saw friends die, became heroes, and then came home to the factories and to vacations at the Dells." I wondered if the soldier in the picture had made it home or not. No way to solve that mystery, I suppose.

I picked up another, older picture. It was of a wedding, with the couple posing together stiffly, their smiles as tight as his collar and her corset. "That one really goes back," the owner said. "They probably hardly knew each other. Heck, this picture probably recorded the first time he'd ever touched her." Suddenly I saw the fear in both their faces. I thought of how mysteriously our world has changed in a century or so . . . or has it really?

A somewhat more recent photo caught my eye. It showed six children, from the oldest and the tallest down to the youngest and the smallest, lined up in their Easter best. The old man pointed out that the cars in the background were from the mid-forties, which was about when I was born. That would make the oldest child about sixty today. I wondered if the children were still living. Was it a picture from a parent's album or from one of theirs? Or maybe it was from an unmarried aunt's. Why hadn't somebody from the family claimed it? Another unsolved mystery.

The last picture was of a baptism, either right before or after the ceremony. The baby, in a christening gown that made it look like a giant tadpole, was being held straight out for the world to see by a young, bearded man and a woman with a feathered hat. They might have been the parents or the godparents. The baby was quite tiny, looking to be only days old. Both the store owner and I decided that this picture had been taken a mighty long time ago.

I turned the picture over. A child had written in pencil, "Me and Uncle Charles and Aunt Lucy." My mind flooded with questions. Was the picture from the estate of someone who attended that person's baptism? What kind of life did this child live? Was it a girl or a boy being held so woodenly? Had baptism made a difference in that person's life? What religion did the family practice? Were their lives happy and fulfilling and blessed by faith? What did Uncle Charles and Aunt Lucy mean to this child? Did they send Christmas presents?

I had too many questions. "You take that one. No charge," the owner said. "No thanks," I replied as I set the picture down. I quickly exited the shop. Too many unsolved questions remained in those pictures. The mystery of life and God's interaction with the people in the pictures was too strong. What mysteries would my own pictures hold? Would I be able to look back at my own pictures someday and see God's grace working in me, or would my life forever be a mystery like the pictures in front of me? Who knows? I felt weighed down. Up the street I saw an electronics store. Sad to say, I felt the need to buy something new and not so mysterious. I ran into the store.

sacred
heart

I FIRMLY BELIEVE THAT ONE OF THE REASONS
I decided to become a priest was that I was a control
freak. While I was quite capable of presenting an
image of faith and trust in God, I honestly needed to
be in control of everything around me. I felt certain
only of the expertise I could bring to a problem, was
confident only in the solution I was capable of offer-
ing. That attitude proved to be extremely dangerous
when I became a pastor.

When all is said and done, so much is really
out of a pastor's control. Running four boilers full
blast through the winter guarantees that, at any one
time, one of them will not be functioning as it
ought. The goal you set with the finance committee
for the weekly collection may not be the same figure
your accountant quotes for all the necessary and
nonnegotiable expenses. Scheduled time off may get
filled with appointments or emergencies. And if you

are not careful, and I wasn't, you will find your life spinning totally out of control.

That is how I ended up flat on my back in the hospital, connected to more monitors than the latest Mars probe. And there is absolutely no out-of-control feeling like the one you experience when you are in the hospital. Everything is controlled by somebody else, from meals to movements (all kinds of movements). Strangers probe you and prod you and examine you and then ask innocently, "Have you heard the bad news?" Add to this some nurses who are too embarrassed to bathe a priest. It made for quite a difficult couple of weeks.

In the course of my stay, the old, trusted family physician decided that it would be good for me to have an angiogram to make sure I had not damaged my heart in any way. But he left the decision up to me. Having been told that it was nothing more than a routine testing procedure, I decided to have it done. My sense of powerlessness kicked in when all of a sudden I was wheeled into what looked suspiciously like an operating theater and was greeted by a team of masked strangers who were calling me by name, although I didn't know any of them.

To make this loss of control complete, I had been given large doses of Valium to calm me down. Perhaps the drug was doing its job, but it was also making me quite weepy. Just before the procedure began, one of the masked strangers asked if I had any questions. Tearfully I asked if they were sure there was film in their camera. I did not want to go through this again. After they finally stopped laughing, I decided it was better to be quiet.

When the test was over and I was resting back in my hospital room, a technician came in and told me that everything was fine. Still pumped up with Valium, I said that I wouldn't believe it until I heard it from my saintly old doctor. Then I started to cry. The doctor finally confirmed it but said he'd send the specialist up to talk to me.

I didn't recognize the specialist without his mask. He brought me to another lab that had an elaborate video monitor. He proceeded to show me the tape they had made of my heart beating. I watched as it showed the dye being injected. He told me how everything had been better than expected. I remained totally silent, so quiet, in fact, that he panicked and asked if I was feeling all right or needed to sit down. (I found out later that someone had written on my chart in red ink: "Patient will ask many questions." Silence was atypical of my behavior.)

I wasn't ill or dizzy. I was awestruck at the sight of my own heart beating. I wordlessly watched those slender vessels and marveled at how the fragility and strength of this creation worked together. The organ that separated life from death was so beautifully ethereal that I could not help but see God's hand in it. What a mysterious and awesome display of God's power and omnipotence.

The doctor asked again what the matter was. I told him how grateful I was for his message that everything was all right. And I realized that he probably viewed hundreds of similar videos every year, but for me, looking at my own heart and its beating had become a spiritual, almost sacramental, moment. The doctor, a devout Hindu, must have understood and asked if I wanted to be alone. I simply nodded, my eyes glued to the screen.

I could not say how long he was gone or how long I watched that video. I do know that I cried. Who knows? Maybe it was still the Valium. But the mystery of God's creation, of God's loving presence being there for me, was stunning. I tried to grasp this mysterious truth: If God had not come for me and loved me and held me, my heart with all its vessels would simply have stopped beating.

There was the other mystery, too, that when my heart *did* someday stop, God's redemptive love for me would be so total that God would call me home to a new life. That realization washed over me. I went back to my hospital room and asked the nurses to hold all phone calls and have my visitors come back later. I just needed some time to be by myself. I found myself remembering my parents' simple devotion to the Sacred Heart of Jesus and the pictures of it around our house.

I was at once grateful and sad, at peace yet filled with questions. It overwhelmed me to be alive here as a mortal while existing in the presence of God. For a few moments I had experienced God as I watched a simple black-and-white video. I needed to absorb that reality and at the same time let go completely—to accept the mystery of God's role in my life and in all life. That experience changed me forever.

gregory

GROWING UP IN A NEIGHBORHOOD OF ALLEYS
meant that we had our own special world of connected gangways, hideouts, porches, and empty lots. It
was a magical place, ruled by us, with all the creativity, freedom, and cruelty our group was capable of.
Because watches were nonexistent luxuries for us,
most of our parents set our time parameters in other
ways. We had to be in by dark or by the time lunch
was on the table. For most of us this was effective
enough in keeping us in line and on the family
schedule. Not so for Gregory. He had it much tougher
than the rest of us. Unfortunately for him, that did
not stop us from making his life even more difficult.

Gregory's artistic family was out of sync with
the rest of the neighborhood. First of all, Gregory's
father worked at home, something unheard of. He
was a restorer of art and a classical painter. He actually used his wife as a model. Gregory's mother was

the only mother in the neighborhood whose nude portrait hung in the living room for everyone to see. Small wonder that we always wanted to visit.

Gregory was also the only kid who had to be in at a specific time during the day. This was for his piano lesson. The rest of us knew that he would be punished if he came home late, and the later he was, the more severe the punishment. No matter what we were doing, if Gregory heard his mother calling him in her singsong voice from their second-story porch, he would drop everything and run home. He knew then that he was late. We knew that, as part of his punishment, he wouldn't get to play with us anymore that day.

Sometimes—when we were playing "war" under the statue of General Sheridan down by the lake—we ended up out of range of Gregory's mother's voice. At those times Gregory's older brother, a classical violinist, would interrupt his own practice, come out on the same porch, and shout Gregory's name, dropping the middle syllable and adding a two-syllable expletive at the end. When Gregory heard that voice, he'd run home faster than we thought possible. We knew he would not be out again, not only that day, but the next as well.

Now, if Gregory was unfortunate enough to get so caught up in our game that he missed the calls of both his mother and his brother, it meant that his father would have to put down his palette. Bare-chested and wearing a beret, he would step imperially onto the porch and bellow Gregory's name, emphasizing the syllable "heh" between "Gre" and "gory." His voice seemed to echo through the canyons of the alleyways. Everyone would stop dead in their tracks. And Gregory would freeze for a moment and then walk home slowly and dejectedly. We said good-bye, not planning to see him for at least a week.

As children, we found this routine curiously amusing. But after a while it became boring, so we decided to spice it up. I confess (not so proudly now) that I learned to imitate Gregory's father's call almost perfectly. And that became the cornerstone of our cruel plan.

First, we got Gregory involved in a new and complex game. When we knew he was into it intensely, I sneaked away, hid under his back porch, and let out my imitation of his father calling him. "Gre-heh-gory" blasted authentically through the neighborhood. Unaware that he had a good two hours before his piano practice, Gregory ran home, leaving all of us bent over in laughter and congratulating one another.

Ten minutes later Gregory came back out, and he was steaming mad. When he saw us standing there in his backyard laughing, he started throwing stones at us. We were too weak from laughing to run away. So we just ducked his wild missiles. I moved out of the way of an unusually large rock that whipped past my left ear, only to hear the crashing sound of the rock breaking the front windshield of the old Chrysler that was Gregory's father's pride and joy.

All laughter stopped. We looked at Gregory and then at each other, and after a split second of standing frozen we all began to run, my friends and I toward our houses and Gregory to who-knows-where. I remember making it to my bed, where I just lay quietly for a good hour or two. All of a sudden I heard the dreaded "Gre-heh-gory." I shuddered. Gregory did not reappear for a month, and then he said nothing and we asked nothing. Life just went on. I never imitated Gregory's father's call again.

God calls us in many ways. This shouldn't frighten us. Unlike human beings, God won't punish us if we have trouble making out the call. At times the message as well as the caller will remain a mystery to us. In fact, there is a good chance that when the call is so clear and so obvious, it won't be God's voice at all. It seems that there is always something unspoken and unclear in what God is asking us to do and to be. We must answer God's call by embracing the mystery.

afterword

SO OFTEN, AFTER I'VE GIVEN A TALK OR
someone has listened to one of my stories, they ask
the inevitable questions: "Did that really happen?"
or "Was that really true?" I am reminded of the great
baseball umpire Jocko Collins, who long after he
retired was quoted as saying, "I never made a wrong
call . . . in my heart." It's the same with my reflections. They are truly the way I remember things . . .
"in my heart." On some points others' recollections
may be different from mine. None of that takes away
from the truth. Such details should never deter us
from telling our stories.

We are in good company, after all. Holy Scripture contains many stories that were first shared
orally before being written down. Imagine the rich-
ness of sitting around a fire and listening to the
account of Noah's flood, shared with all its warmth,
its drama, and its humor. How thrilling it must have

been for those early Christians who gathered to break bread together in Jesus' memory to hear the story of Jesus' miracles. How amazing to hear the words of his sayings handed down through the reflections of the apostles who knew him intimately.

Our reflections are made sacred when we connect them to the story of our faith.

Once after I preached a Lenten mission in a parish outside of Chicago, the pastor, trying to pay me a compliment, said that he wished he had stories like mine to tell. Imagine saying that after being a minister of Christ for a third of a century! I told him that he did have stories to tell. He needed only to begin searching his heart to find them. Once we begin to share our stories, they pour out like a newly tapped spring.

I have been privileged to bump into God unexpectedly because of so many wonderful and interesting people in my life. Let me thank all of you who, by sharing yourselves with me, have graced my life so incredibly. Your stories have become a part of my story. To my family and friends whose stories have intertwined with my life and my ministry—for your support and love I give thanks. These stories are especially for you.

bumping into *God* again

$15.95 U.S. Hardcover
0-8294-1510-6

LOYOLAPRESS.

3441 N. Ashland Ave.
Chicago, IL 60657

PHONE 800.621.1008
FAX 773.281.0555
www.loyolapress.org

66 *Grassi finds evidence of God's will, God's love, God's forgiveness, God's mystery, and God's sense of humor.* 99

—The New World

Bumping into God Again gives us more stories that magnify, in simple and powerful ways, God's grace all around us. Dominic Grassi narrates another collection of anecdotes, revealing God in everyday people, places, and things.